Confidence in Christ

An Engineer's Examination of the Physical Evidence for Christ

Mike Bradfield

WESTBOW PRESS®
A DIVISION OF THOMAS NELSON & ZONDERVAN

WestBow Press books may be ordered through booksellers or by contacting:

WestBow Press
A Division of Thomas Nelson & Zondervan
1663 Liberty Drive
Bloomington, IN 47403
www.westbowpress.com
1 (866) 928-1240

ISBN: 978-1-9736-2681-7 (sc)
ISBN: 978-1-9736-2680-0 (hc)
ISBN: 978-1-9736-2682-4 (e)

Library of Congress Control Number: 2018904932

Print information available on the last page.

WestBow Press rev. date: 05/22/2018

Contents

Introduction vii

1. **How Did It All Begin?** 1
   13.8 to 8.3 Billion Years BC: Bible Day 1
2. **Creating the Perfect Biosphere for Life** 15
   8.3 to 0.86 Billion Years BC: Bible Days 2-4
3. **How Did Life Begin?** 28
   860 to 250 Million Years BC: Bible Days 5-6
4. **Are We Physically Evolved Apes?** 48
   250 Million Years to 4000 BC: Bible Day 6
5. **Are We Spiritually Evolved Apes?** 65
   4000 BC: Bible Day 6
6. **What Yom Is It?** 76
   13.8 Billion Years to 4000 BC: Bible Days 1-6
7. **Old Testament–Era Evidence** 95
   4000 BC to 400 BC
8. **Prophecies on Jesus** 131
   4000 BC to 400 BC
9. **New Testament-Era Evidence** 155
   4 BC–AD 60
10. **Did the Resurrection Really Happen?** 185
    AD 30

11. What Have Others Written about Jesus? 198
AD 52 to AD 140

12. Is Jesus the Christ? 214

Acknowledgments 227
Table of Figures 229
Endnotes 233

Introduction

> But these are written that you may believe that Jesus is the Christ, the Son of God, and that by believing you may have life in his name.
>
> John 20:31

As a young engineer, I had the opportunity to travel to Paris, France, where we were preparing to manufacture a new product I had designed. On one such trip, an older colleague of mine was on his morning commute from the Grand Hotel in Paris to the manufacturing plant. He grew up in the heart of the Midwest, and English was his only language. While among French-speaking people in France, his ears and mind conditioned themselves to tune out external conversations since he could not decipher what they were saying. He did not realize how much so until one particular morning. On that day, a well-suited French businessman boarded the elevator with him as he rode down to the lobby. On the way down, the French businessman looked at him and said, "Sir, I like your tie." My colleague nodded and smiled but made no remark back. The elevator descended a few more floors as passengers shuffled in and out of the elevator.

The French businessman, attempting to start a conversation with him again, said, "Sir, I like your tie."

My colleague responded in English, "I'm sorry, I don't speak French."

To this the French businessman responded, "Sir, I am speaking to you in English!"

Figure i.1: Speaking the same language without realizing it

This is how I see our present situation regarding the Christian faith. The theologians and scientists are saying the same thing, but very few realize it. Through the years, many have tuned each other out and consequently do not recognize they are saying the same thing. This book is an attempt to speak the language of both the theologians and scientists to show just how closely the Christian faith and modern science are aligned.

As an engineer, I embrace and uphold science and the scientific method to study the world around us. Although science does not always get it right the first time, over time as the scientific body of knowledge for a particular subject or topic grows and understanding deepens, it tends to be self-correcting. Theories and ideas in error are either improved or corrected as needed or are abandoned totally if necessary. For example, we do not think the rest of the universe revolves around the earth as once was widely held by the scientific community. Rather, we know that within our solar system, the earth revolves around the sun.

As science has self-corrected over time and drawn closer to the absolute truth, science has drawn closer and closer to the steadfast word of God as expressed in the Bible. As we will see, science is currently standing on the threshold of Christianity and knocking on the door. It is time to open the door, examine the evidence, and embrace Christ confidently.

Chapter 1

How Did It All Begin?

13.8 to 8.3 Billion Years BC: Bible Day 1

I have a curiosity about the world around us, and how things work has always intrigued me. When I was growing up, my dad was patient in answering my many curious questions. Seeking his affirmation on various thoughts on subjects, I would state, "Huh, Dad?" which was usually followed by his response, "That's right!" Christmas could be especially trying for my parents' patience and understanding. Often to me the best part about new toys was not playing with them for the first time Christmas morning. Rather, it was tearing them apart and disassembling them in the afternoon to find out how they worked and what made them tick. Nuts, bolts, gears, electric motors, electrical circuits, housings—so many interesting things, so little time.

Coupled with my insatiable curiosity, which raised havoc with my Christmas toys and whatever else my hands could get ahold of before my parents would stop me from disassembling it, I also have always had a love of math and science. Looking back, there should have been little doubt what my future career would be. When I learned about engineering as a sophomore in high school, there was no doubt this was the profession for me. Since that time, I have never look back or regretted the decision. Now meetings, time charts, paperwork, and evaluations are just nuisances blocking the way of pursuing my real passion: using those childhood learnings coupled with an engineering education to create new, innovative products. It is Christmas every day! Well … some days.

But my curiosity didn't stop within my engineering world. It also spilled over into my spiritual world. Where did the universe come from? Is there a God? How do we know that the Bible is really God's word? Did Jesus really come back to life after being dead? A whole litany of other related questions filled my mind. However, unlike my engineering world where answers could be physically or mathematically determined, such as through a controlled experiment, issues of the spiritual realm are not as easy to determine. Or so I thought. How do you run a spiritual experiment where you control all the variables except for one, say God, and then turn God on and off and observe the effect on the rest of the system? Or how do we prove the Bible is God's word?

When I was young, I thought these types of matters were outside of scientific study and proof. You just had to take them on faith. The truth is, God wants us to come to him in faith, and without faith you cannot please God. This is per his plan and word, the Bible. But our faith does not have to be blind or without foundation. As I have learned through the years by continually digging and seeking God, there is an extensive amount of scientific evidence God has given us supporting the Christian faith. The further and deeper my curiosity drove me to dig into fact-based support of Christianity, the broader and deeper the evidence has become. I have also come to realize just as science and technology are exploding, right in step with these developments is the growth in scientific evidence for God and Christianity.

So where do we start, or how do we start, and then how do we proceed? In typical engineering linear logic fashion, we will just start at the beginning of time and then simply flow through time chronologically and examine some of the evidence along the way. So let's go back—way back—to the beginning of time.

Beginning of Time: 13.8 Billion Years Ago—Day 1

The boldfaced date shown here for the beginning of time, and all boldfaced dates throughout this book, should not be interpreted as exact dates. The nature of the item or event and the available data concerning them precludes exact dating. Boldfaced dates are based on sources referenced throughout the book.

Without any fanfare, the Bible starts off straightforwardly by giving us an account of God's creation of the universe:

> In the beginning God created the heavens and the earth. Now the earth was formless and empty, darkness was over the surface of the deep, and the Spirit of God was hovering over the waters. And God said, "Let there be light," and there was light. God saw that the light was good, and he separated the light from the darkness. God called the light "day", and the darkness he called "night." And there was evening, and there was morning—the first day. (Genesis 1:1–5)

From this, we learn the Bible teaches that before the start of time, there were no planets, no earth, no animals, and no humans. Just God. Per the Christian faith, God is eternal. He has no beginning or ending. He has always existed. Only things with a beginning need to be made. Since God was not made, he had no beginning. God, the great "I Am," has always existed.

We also learn from the first few verses in the Bible that the universe had a finite, definite beginning. The physical universe did not exist prior to God creating it. God is the outside source responsible for the creation of the universe.

Was Jesus present at this time? Absolutely. Jesus, who is God incarnate, or God in the flesh, is the Creator. From the book of John in the Bible we read:

> In the beginning was the Word, and the Word was with God, and the Word was God. He was with God in the beginning. Through him all things were made; without him nothing was made that has been made. (John 1:1–3)

Jesus is known throughout the Bible as the "Word of God." From this passage, we learn Jesus, who was God in human form, was there at the beginning and through him all things were made. Therefore, Jesus was present at the beginning since he is the Creator.

Now that we have briefly examined what the Christian faith has to say about the initial beginning of the universe, let's turn to science and allow it to weigh in with the latest understanding of the beginning of the universe. Understand, though, science is not absolute or infallible. It is based on observations, and interpretations of those observations can be biased. Two people can look at the same body of evidence and arrive at two diametrically opposed conclusions based on their worldviews of whether God exists.

In the case of the beginning of the universe, let's first draw on engineering and the first law of thermodynamics. The first law of thermodynamics states that for a closed or open system, energy is conserved. Energy cannot be created or destroyed; it can only change forms. This is often loosely referred to as the law of "cause and effect." For every created effect, there is a cause.

Consider a hypothetical sealed, closed box the size of a microwave that does not allow any energy or matter to enter in or escape out. In its original state, it is empty and void. Now suppose once a day we peer inside the box without disturbing the void in the box itself. Day after day we observe absolutely nothing in the box. Then one day we peer in and are surprised to see a coffee pot, coffee cups, saucers, and hot coffee in the pot itself. What would we conclude? We would probably conclude an external cause, or source, put the material inside the box. This would be consistent with the first law of thermodynamics.

Figure 1.1: Sealed box with coffee setting

Uncountable experiments through the years have upheld this theory, and all attempts to find an exception to this law have failed. The first law of thermodynamics is a very time-tested theory.

Now consider a much larger box. And this time instead of a coffee setting, we observe the whole universe. Again, what would we conclude? The first law of thermodynamics would again suggest an external cause is responsible for all the matter and energy present. Hold that thought for a moment, and let's move on to the second law of thermodynamics.

Figure 1.2: Sealed box with universe inside

The second law of thermodynamics states all processes increase the disorder, or entropy, of the system. What does this mean? It means the total energy is constant, per the first law of thermodynamics, but the quality or availability of the energy to do useful work decreases. In layman's terms, real, natural processes always bring about a decay.

The second law of thermodynamics can be observed in the first experiment with the coffee pot. Suppose we observe the coffee setting over a period of time and could measure the temperature of the various elements inside the box without disturbing the system. What we would observe is the coffee would cool down and the coffee pot, coffee cups, saucers, and whatever gas is within the box would heat up slightly. Over time all the elements would reach the same temperature. This temperature would be lower than the original coffee temperature. By the first law, the energy inside the box would stay constant throughout this time, but the availability of the energy, or its ability to do useful work, would decrease in observance of the second law of thermodynamics due to the cooling of the coffee.

Now consider the second experiment again, where we observed the universe inside our box. What is happening in the universe over time? Decay. The energy of our sun and other suns in the universe is being dispersed through space. The earth's magnetic field and rotation are decaying. Eventually the universe will decay and die from the lack of available heat energy from the sun. Since the universe is decaying, it must have had a beginning. But since the universe is not dead yet, we can also deduce it cannot be infinitely old.

Another area supporting this notion comes from the decay of radioactive elements present in the earth's crust. Radioactive elements such as uranium and thorium are decaying and will eventually turn to lead. Their existence and observable decay tell us the atoms are not infinitely old. This indicates the earth itself had a definite beginning.

Therefore, when we apply the first two laws of thermodynamics together to our universe, it suggests, from the first law, that the universe could not begin by itself, and from the second law, the universe had a beginning. Again, the universe has a beginning brought out by an external cause and is not infinitely old and static.

Now let's turn our attention to astronomy. What do the latest astronomical and cosmological understandings indicate concerning the origin of matter? To start off, we need to dig down a bit into the theory of relativity as revealed by Albert Einstein.

Figure 1.3: Albert Einstein

Einstein's original work describing the relationships of space-time was published in 1905.[1] He later expanded the theory to include the gravitational effects that could be applied in a general sense (i.e., to the universe). His field equations describe the fundamental interactions of gravity due to space-time being curved by matter and energy. Although the equations look simple enough, they involve sixteen complex partial differential equations.

The "relativity" in his theory comes from the fact that the reference frame for an observation is vital to understanding the measured results. For instance, suppose two people are put inside a cardboard box and then placed on the ground. When asked what forces they feel, they would respond they feel a force on their bodies pulling them downward. From a vantage point outside the box, we would observe this is due to the gravity of the earth. Now suppose instead of being placed on the ground, they and the cardboard box are loaded aboard a spaceship. At a distance far from the gravitational field of any planet, the spaceship accelerates. Now suppose the acceleration rate of the rocket exactly matches that of the acceleration due to gravity at the earth's surface. When asked what force they felt, they would respond they felt the exact same force as before pulling them downward. From a vantage point outside of the box, we would observe this is due to the acceleration of the spaceship. So even though the mechanism was completely different, the actual force and force sensation would be the same and the observer inside the box could not tell the difference. Understanding the reference frame for the measurement is vital in understanding the observation.

One area of unique phenomenon associated with Einstein's theory of relativity, and this issue of reference frame, is time dilation. As predicted by his theory, large massive bodies, such as planets, that create gravity and travel at speeds near the speed of light, warp time. If you are near a large, massive body, the gravitational effect slows down time. Similarly, traveling at an extremely high speed also slows down time. Like the simple example above, time is completely dependent on your reference frame. Time elapses differently at each position throughout the universe. Two identical clocks, one on Earth and another on Mars, would record different elapsed times. Later when we consider time dilation during the first six days of creation, we will see where we place the "clock" to establish the reference frame is vital to the observed measurement of time.

If at this point you are thinking the theory of relativity and this issue of time dilation are just theories, think again. They have been proven again and again throughout the world. In fact, Einstein's theory of relativity could really be called the law of relativity in line with other scientifically observed correlations, such as gravity itself. One such experiment by Hafele and Keating in 1971 involved four cesium beam atomic clocks.[2] They synchronized the four clocks with stationary atomic clocks at the US Naval Observatory and then flew the clocks around the earth twice, first traveling eastward and then on the second trip, westward. When the four clocks were compared to the stationary control clocks, the shift following the eastward and westward flights was in accordance with the theory of relativity as it accounts for the changes in gravity, relative speed, and direction of rotation.

An everyday practical example of Einstein's theory concerns GPS in cell phones. They receive their information from satellites circling high above the earth. Because of the difference in gravity and therefore time, this time dilation must be accounted for as predicted by the theory of relativity. If you are wondering how much the correction is, if it was not accounted for, your GPS would accumulate a location error of over six miles every day.[3] Relativity and time dilation are not theories; they are real, proven scientific phenomenon. They are repeatable, measurable, and predictable.

When Einstein applied the theory of relativity to the whole universe, an interesting result came forth; the universe was not static as commonly thought. It had to be either expanding or contracting. But if the universe was changing in size, and not statically remaining the same as thought, this implied a beginning. And a beginning implied a beginner—God.

Einstein realized this and doubted the results of his own work. He was an atheist at this time, and the prevailing scientific thought was that the universe was static and to suggest otherwise was heresy. This led Einstein to do the scientifically unthinkable. He actually added a fudge factor into his equation, called a cosmological constant, and set its value such that when the equations were solved, the universe remained static. Unthinkable, yet true. This speaks volumes to the bias that can enter into scientific work, even by those who are held in the highest regard. Undoubtedly Einstein is one of the greatest scientists of all times. You would expect the results and conclusions from his scientific work to reflect the highest integrity.

Not so. He caved in to his own atheist bias and peer pressure and distorted his own theory.

Fortunately, history usually gets things right, and science tends to be self-correcting. In this case it happened as well. Other scientists around the world picked up on Einstein's work and detected something was amiss with his cosmological constant prediction of a static universe. First was American astronomer Vesto Slipher in 1914.[4] He discovered all galaxies were receding from us at high velocities. Then, in 1922, Russian mathematician Alexander Friedman discovered Einstein's static universe was impossible based on the relativity equations.[5] This was followed by a Belgian physicist Georges Lemaitre in 1927, who reached the same conclusion as Friedman.[6] Finally, in 1929, American astronomer Edwin Hubble who was studying the red shifting of planets and distant galaxies discovered the universe was not merely expanding; it was exploding.[7]

In response, Einstein traveled to the United States and visited with Edwin Hubble and others at his observatory in Pasadena, California, in 1931. There, while looking through the world's most powerful telescope at that time, Einstein saw for himself the evidence in the planets showing the universe was not static, but rapidly expanding. This in turn meant there was a beginning to the universe, and a beginning meant a creator. Einstein corrected his error and called it "the biggest blunder [he] ever made."[8] It is worth noting that after this occurred, Einstein believed in a creator God.

The term *big bang* originated years later by Sir Fred Hoyle in 1950 on an English BBC radio broadcast as a sarcastic remark. He was a proponent of the steady-state universe and said, "The big bang theory requires a recent origin of the Universe that openly invites the concept of creation," something he did not believe in himself.[9] Through his studies, however, he later stubbornly embraced the big bang theory and its implications.

Up until 1965, the big bang theory was just that—a theory. In that year it all changed and somewhat by accident. In that year two physicists at AT&T Bell Laboratories in New Jersey found the predicted remnant of the big bang.[10] While working to refine the world's most sensitive radio listening device, they kept picking up an unknown source of noise corresponding to a temperature of around three degrees Kelvin. At first they thought it was bird droppings on their antenna, but later it was identified as remnant background radiation from the big bang, thus proving its occurrence. In essence, they proved the first three words of the Christian Bible are true, "In the beginning." Now with 791,328 words in the King James Bible, we only have 791,325 words to go![11]

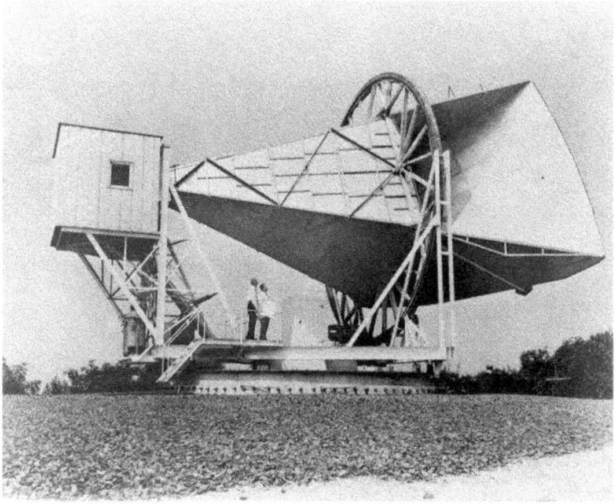

Figure 1.4: Physicists Robert Wilson and Arno Penzias with their radio listening device in 1965

Another discovery giving credibility to the big bang theory occurred in 1990. NASA's Cosmic Background Explorer (COBE) confirmed the background radiation had the exact match for a blackbody curve exactly as predicted by the big bang theory.[12]

Still another source of evidence for the big bang comes from the origin of light elements like helium.[13] Helium requires extremely high temperatures, millions of degrees, to form. The only known mechanism plausible is the extreme, intense heat that would have been present during the big bang.

So, according to the big bang, how did everything come into existence? The entire universe was initially an incredibly hot single point, or singularity, of extreme energy. An external cause outside of this singularity caused it to expand. In an extremely small period of time, much less than a second, a period of hyper expansion occurred, and the universe grew many times over. As it expanded, it became cooler and less dense. It did not explode, as implied by the term big bang, but rather expanded rapidly, much like a balloon being rapidly inflated. The universe is like the surface of the balloon, and not a volume like the interior of the balloon. And like a balloon, the galaxies of the universe are like dots on the surface of the balloon, continually getting farther apart as the balloon inflates. The expansion of the universe continues to this day, with the expansion rate occurring near the speed of light, 186,000 miles per second.[14] During this initial time, the earth was a formless ball of swirling gas. At some point during this initial subsecond period of time as the temperature of the universe cooled due to the expansion, electrons bonded with atomic nuclei, producing light.

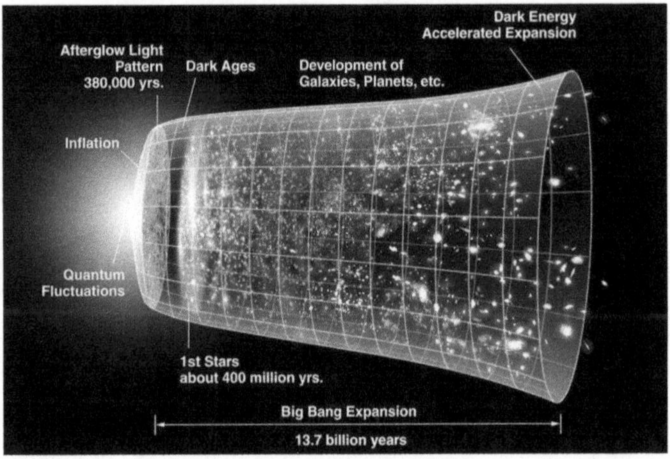

Figure 1.5: NASA's graphic representation of the big bang and expansion of the universe[15]

So in summary, what is the current mainstream scientific thought regarding the origin of the universe?

1) The first and second laws of thermodynamics indicate the universe had a finite beginning brought about by an external cause.
2) Decaying radioactive materials on the earth further indicate the universe had a beginning and is not infinitely old.
3) The big bang, and its overwhelming supportive data, is the current mainstream scientific explanation of the beginning of the universe. The big bang indicates the universe started as a single point or singularity. There was no light, just intense energy. An external cause precipitated the expansion of this single point, and after a very short period of time, as the universe cooled due to expansion, light elements such as helium and hydrogen would have formed and then light itself would have appeared for the first time.

What does the Bible say regarding the origin of the universe? You may want to reread Genesis 1:1–5 from the start of this chapter. Genesis states that in the beginning there was only God. God is not a created being, and therefore he had no beginning. At the start of time, God was the external cause that precipitated the expansion of the singularity into the physical universe:

> In the beginning, God created the heavens and the earth. (Genesis 1:1)

Originally the earth was a swirling ball of gas:

> Now the earth was formless and empty, darkness was over the surface of the deep. (Genesis 1:2)

Due to the extreme concentration of matter and therefore

extreme gravity, light itself couldn't escape the gravitational pull. But after a period of time, as the universe expanded, the gravitational pull became much less, the temperature became much less, and atomic bonds began to form and light was emitted:

> And God said, "Let there be light," and there was light. (Genesis 1:3)

Moses is credited with writing these words in the first book of the Bible, Genesis, around 1445 BC.[16] He correctly identified an external cause, "God," who created the universe at a very definite point in time, "in the beginning," the earth was initially "formless and empty," followed by the emergence of light, "Let there be light." All in perfect agreement with modern scientific thought. Coincidence?

Chapter 2

Creating the Perfect Biosphere for Life

8.3 to 0.86 Billion Years BC: Bible Days 2-4

It is funny how certain things remain frozen in our minds and how we can recall vivid details many years later. Such is the case with my freshman engineering orientation class at college. All the incoming freshman with a declared major of mechanical engineering were shuttled into a large lecture hall. When everybody settled in and with almost all the seats filled, we were given "the speech" by the department chair. After several introductory topics, he instructed us to look left and then right at the students sitting next to us. He then proceeded to tell us although he would dearly like to see all of us succeed in engineering, statistically only one of us would graduate. Gulp! The cold hard truth can sometimes be just that, cold and hard. For many in the room, it was a big wake-up call.

As low as those odds seemed back then, I have come to realize it is nothing compared to the odds that our universe and laws of nature just randomly happened. Our universe and laws of nature are fine-tuned beyond belief. Just an incredibly slightly smaller or larger value for gravity and there would be no life on earth. Just an incredibly slightly slower or higher expansion rate for the formation of the universe, and not only would there be no life, there would be no universe. This is not a "look to the planet to the left and right of us and only one of you will remain." No, this is an all or nothing. Just a very small value to the basic forces of nature such as gravity, and nothing exists. So let's dig into the formation of the universe and see how it is finely tuned and balanced.

After the initial start of matter and time during day 1, the Bible describes how God went about creating the perfect biosphere for life: earth. Following the initial hyper-inflationary period, the universe continued to expand, and still does today, near the astonishing speed of light. This expansion of the universe is one of the fundamental mechanisms leading to the creation of the universe and earth from the initial infinitesimally small ball of extreme energy and heat. Beyond the creation account given in Genesis, there are passages throughout the Bible relating to the creation of the universe and the stretching out of the universe at the hand of God. The following is a listing of some of them:

> He stretches out the heavens like a canopy.
> (Isaiah 40:22)

> He who created the heavens and stretched them out.
> (Isaiah 42:5)

> Who has made all things, who alone stretched out the heavens.
> (Isaiah 44:24)

> My own hands stretched out the heavens.
> (Isaiah 45:12)

> And my right hand spread out the heavens.
> (Isaiah 48:13)

> the Lord your Maker, who stretched out the heavens.
> (Isaiah 51:13)

> And stretched out the heavens by his understanding.
> (Jeremiah 10:12)

> He spreads out the northern skies over empty space.
> (Job 26:7)

> Can you join him spreading out the skies?
> (Job 37:18)

> He stretches out the heavens like a tent.
> (Psalm 104:5)

These passages correctly imply the universe was not created at its present size, but rather the universe is being expanded and stretched. Also note the use of the terms *canopy* and *tent*, which aligns with the scientific understanding of our universe that it is more like a surface rather than a volume.

8.3 Billion Years Ago: Day 2

Now let's look at the biblical and scientific account of the events that took place during this early expansion that led to the creation of the universe and earth.

> And God said, "Let there be an expanse between the waters to separate water from water." So God made the expanse and separated the water under the expanse from the water above it. And it was so. God called the expanse "sky." And there was evening and there was morning—the second day. (Genesis 1:6–8)

Per the big bang theory, from the swirling gaseous clouds, galaxies started to form, including the disk of our own Milky Way. As the universe continued to expand, it continued to cool. Initially this cooling from the extraordinarily hot condition allowed atoms to form from the conversion of energy to mass. Continued expansion of the universe and cooling of the created matter allowed some of the matter to change phase from gaseous to liquid. This caused the creation and separation of the heavier elements into liquid and the lighter elements to remain a gas. This is in perfect agreement with the Bible.

4.5 Billion Years Ago: Day 3

> And God said, "Let the water under the sky be gathered to one place, and let dry ground appear." And it was so. God called the dry ground "land," and the gathered waters he called "seas." And God saw that it was good. Then God said, "Let the land produce vegetation: seed-bearing plants and trees on the land that bear fruit with seed in it, according to their various kinds." And it was so. The land produced vegetation: plants bearing seed according to their kinds. And God saw that it was good. And there was evening, and there was morning—the third day. (Genesis 1:9–13)

Per the big bang theory and latest scientific thought, the swirling, gaseous cloud that is to become earth cools and solidifies. Earth comes into existence as a planet during this time. Earth continues to cool, and liquid water appears. The water vapor of the atmosphere separates from the liquid water of earth. Dry ground on earth appears due to plate movement and volcanic activity. A heavy cloud cover envelops earth. Visible light from the sun is not present on earth, but some level of ultraviolet light penetrates the cloud cover, and as soon as liquid water is present, plant life emerges.

Figure 2.1: Earth

2.2 Billion Years Ago: Day 4

> And God said, "Let there be lights in the expanse of the sky to separate the day from the night, and let them serve as signs to mark seasons and days and years, and let them be lights in the expanse of the sky to give light on the earth." And it was so. God made two great lights—the greater light to govern the day and the lesser light to govern the night. He also made the stars. God set them in the expanse of the sky to give light on the earth, to govern the day and the night, and to separate light from darkness. And God saw that it was good. And there was evening, and there was morning—the fourth day. (Genesis 1:14–19)

Due to the plant life now on the earth, photosynthesized oxygenation of the atmosphere occurred and reached a level comparable to today's earth environment. With the combination of the continued cooling of the earth, the rise in atmospheric oxygen, and the volcanic ash settling, the cloud cover begins to clear. The sun and the moon, which were already formed but not visible due to the cloud cover, now become visible from the earth.

Again, the agreement between the latest scientific thoughts per the big bang theory and the Christian Bible on the origin and development of the universe and the earth is uncanny. How could Moses writing thirty-five hundred years ago accurately describe the formation of the universe without some form of divine guidance? Keep in mind, this is thousands of years before humankind had a basic understanding of the universe, such as that the earth was not the center of the universe.

Before we proceed, it is worth stopping for a moment to consider what has been created up to this point by the end of day 4. Consider first the atom, life's simplest building block. Atoms were created when the incredibly hot, single point of energy, the singularity, expanded and became mass, atoms, and light, per Einstein's famous equation of energy equals mass times the speed of light squared ($E = mc^2$). The atom itself consists of neutrons, protons, and electrons. The relative mass between neutrons, protons, and electrons is finely balanced, as is the charge of the electron. Just an extremely small change in any of these properties and the world would not exist because molecules could not form. How could you explain the creation of atoms through evolutionary processes? Trial and error through evolutionary processes will not create an atom. The composition and charges of its components must be exactly right all at once initially or it cannot come into existence. There is no stair-stepping process leading to its creation. It's an all-or-nothing design.

Now consider the extremely precise setting of the resonance of life-enabling carbon. The resonance (energy level) of the carbon nucleus must be precisely set for life, enabling carbon to exist. Just an extremely small change in this level, higher or lower, would not permit carbon to exist. And without carbon, there is no life.

Before physicists found the resonance of carbon, Fred Hoyle (who coined the term big bang) precisely predicted what it should be based solely on life's need for it. Hoyle, an atheist, took the uncanny approach of asking what God would have set the energy level at to permit life. Hoyle left his home in Cambridge, England, for a period of time to teach and research at Cal Tech. While there he was able to convince researchers to test for the resonance of carbon to confirm his theory. Much to their surprise when it was finally tested, Hoyle had nailed it exactly.[1]

In the November 1981 issue of *Engineering and Science* Fred Hoyle quipped,

> A common sense interpretation of the facts suggest that a super intellect has monkeyed with physics, as well as with chemistry and biology, and that there are no blind forces worth speaking about in nature. The number one calculates from the facts seem to me so overwhelming as to put this conclusion almost beyond question.[2]

Now consider the relative strengths of nature's four forces: gravity, electromagnetism, strong nuclear forces, and weak nuclear forces. These four forces are finely balanced to allow the formation of atoms and planets and life itself. Any very slight variation in any of these forces and life itself would not be possible.

Further, consider the planetary force balance. Just as the relative strengths of nature's four forces are finely tuned, enabling atoms to exist, the balance between gravitational force and electromagnetic force also enables stars to exist. The gravitational force holds the stars together, and the electromagnetic force allows the stars to radiate energy. If the balance were not right, then stars would either be red giants or blue dwarfs, making it impossible to sustain human life. This balance is one part in 10^{40}.[3]

Still further, consider the universe's expansion and collapse.

The expansion force of our universe is precisely balanced by the gravitational force, allowing galaxies to form but not enough to come crashing back into itself. The fine-tuning of the cosmological constant has been estimated to be one part in 10^{55}.[4] This extreme fine-tuning of the world around us has led Robin Collins, professor of philosophy at Messiah College, to state, "Over the past thirty years or so, scientists have discovered that just about everything about the basic structure of the universe is balanced on a razor's edge for life to exist. The coincidences are far too fantastic to attribute this to mere chance or to claim that it needs no explanation. The dials are set too precisely to have been a random accident."[5] Even renowned physicist and atheist Stephen Hawking commented, "The remarkable fact is that the values of these numbers seem to have been very finely adjusted to make possible the development of life."[6]

Now consider the earth's biosphere. There are many physical and cosmological parameters that must be set to extreme precision to allow life on earth to be possible, such as earth's location, size, composition, structure, atmosphere, and temperature, as well as earth's intricate cycles such as the carbon cycle, oxygen cycle, and nitrogen cycle. Extremely small variations in the parameter settings make the biosphere uninhabitable and void of life. It is uncanny and unnatural the precision of these settings, and there is no natural explanation for their settings. The logical conclusion is some intelligent being or force created the biosphere with all the right conditions and properties to sustain life.

Finally, consider the whole universe. One theory to explain intelligent design and the ultra-precision of various physical and biological constants is the concept of many universes. With many possible universes, we are just one of the lucky planets at the right place at the right time where all the dials were set correctly to support life. In other words, we are one of the lucky cosmic lottery winners. However, under further scrutiny, astronomers are starting to cast serious doubt on this proposition as well. It looks more like we may be the *only* lucky cosmic winner within our universe.

Carl Sagan, the well-known astronomer who hosted the *Cosmos* TV programs of the 1970s, had this to say concerning the possibility of life on other planets based on different elements:

> No other chemical element comes close to carbon in the variety and intricacy of the compounds it can form; liquid water provides a superb, stable medium in which organic molecules can dissolve and interact ... Certain atoms, such as silicon, might be able to take on some of the roles of carbon in an alternative life chemistry, but the variety of information-bearing molecules they provide seem comparatively sparse. Furthermore, the silicon equivalent of carbon dioxide is, on all planetary surfaces, a solid, not a gas. That distinction would certainly complicate the development of a silicon-based metabolism. For the moment, carbon and water-based life forms are the only kinds we know or can even imagine.[7]

What Sagan and other scientists are saying is that only a carbon-based life is imaginable. Further, life requires water in liquid form. When these two factors are put together, the potential places in our universe having these two elements shrinks drastically.

Now consider the work of Dr. Guillermo Gonzalez. Dr. Gonzalez is a world-class astronomer who has studied the potential habitable zones in the cosmos. His findings are discussed in the book he coauthored with Dr. Jay Richards titled *The Privileged Planet*.[8]

Gonzalez explains that there are three types of galaxies. First are the globular cluster galaxies. As the name suggests, the general shape of this galaxy is globular. These galaxies contain the most ancient stars. They consist of almost all hydrogen and helium. The elements needed for life, such as carbon, oxygen, and nitrogen, appear only in low levels. There are no accompanying planets around the stars in a globular cluster like the earth, only dust, grains, or boulders. Finally, the densely packed stars do not allow stable circular orbits, and this results in extreme climate variation. The conclusion is globular cluster galaxies would not support life, so scratch them off the potential life-supporting areas.

Next are elliptical galaxies. Most galaxies are elliptical and resemble the general shape of an egg. The elliptical shape does not provide safe harbors for life also due to extreme climate changes. The exploding supernovas throughout would inhibit life. There are also gamma ray bursts more powerful than a supernova. The conclusion is, elliptical galaxies, like globular clusters, would not support life.

This leads us finally to spiral galaxies. Spiral galaxies do indeed provide potential safe zones for life, but only in their mid-zone. The center nucleus of the galaxy contains dangerous and massive black holes where high levels of dangerous energy is released in the form of gamma rays, X-rays, and particle radiation. There are also many supernovas exploding at the nucleus of a spiral galaxy. Likewise, out on the arms of the spirals, there are supernovas exploding. An eccentric orbit would cause a planet to travel through the dangerous spiral arms and inner regions. However, the thin disk shape of the spiral galaxies creates desirable circular orbits to keep planets within a safe, life-enabling, habitable mid-zone.

Figure 2.2: Artist rendering of Milky Way

Not surprisingly, the Milky Way in which we live in is a spiral galaxy. The Milky Way is in the top 1 to 2 percent of the most massive and luminous galaxies.[9] This mass helps to create heavy elements needed for life. Jupiter, which is thee hundred times more massive than Earth, acts as a shield to protect Earth from comet impacts.[10] Other planets, from Mars to Jupiter, also shield us from asteroids. The position of Earth in relation to the sun is exactly where life-sustaining water can exist on the surface of the planet in liquid form as determined by the amount of light and heat from the sun. There is a really fine line between low enough carbon dioxide levels required to maintain an atmosphere to have liquid and yet high enough oxygen levels to maintain life. Earth has exactly the right balance. If Earth was closer or farther from the sun, there would be no life. Earth's very circular orbit is also critical to minimize temperature variations.

Now consider the sun. Nuclear fusion occurring at the sun 93 million miles away provides us warmth and energy.[11] Our sun is in the top 10 percent most massive stars in the galaxy, and its size permits life.[12] Most stars are red dwarfs and emit light in the red part of the spectrum. Photosynthesis is less efficient in this mostly red variation. If the sun were smaller, planets would have to orbit closer (due to lower gravity), eventually becoming tidally locked, whereby they always face the sun in the same direction. Flares would also be a problem with smaller stars because of being too close and the resulting temperature spikes. Too massive of a sun and there would be excessive blue radiation. Like red light, this is also bad for photosynthesis. Stars just a little more massive than our sun do not live long. The sun's output is very stable, varying by only 0.1 percent over a full sunspot cycle of eleven years, which is also important for sustaining life on earth.[13] Our sun's orbit is also more circular than other stars in our galaxy, which keeps Earth in a safe zone. In short, our sun is perfectly sized to enable life on earth.

Now let's examine the moon. The prevalent scientific theory is the moon was formed by a glancing collision with a Mars-sized body during Earth's later stage of formation.[14] The moon is essential to our stable, life-enabling climate. In 1993 it was discovered that the moon stabilizes the tilt of the earth's axis, and the earth's tilt governs seasons.[15] The moon also contributes 60 percent to the tides in the oceans, with the sun providing the other 40 percent.[16] These lunar- or moon-induced tides maintain large-scale circulation of the oceans. This is important because the ocean carries heat and acts as a large thermal buffer for earth to keep climates moderate. If the moon were larger, the tides would be too large, and it would slow down the rotation of earth too much. The moon is just the right size. Since moons play an essential role in creating a stable climate and moon-forming collisions are rare throughout the universe, habitable planets are therefore also rare.

The earth, our solar system, and the Milky Way galaxy were once thought of as very ordinary and mundane and there was nothing special about them. Now, scientists are realizing just how extraordinarily special the life-bearing earth really is. The earth is the very rare exception, not the norm. It appears that our planetary system was precisely and uniquely designed to support life on earth. The hottest issue cosmologists grapple with today is not, "Is there intelligent life on other planets?" but rather, "Why is earth so hospitable to life in the first place, and who or what intelligence created it?"

All this evidence suggests that matter, the planets, and the universe could not have been created by naturalistic causes. Our perfect biosphere for life, earth, simply could not have happened by random chances and naturalistic causes. Throughout our entire universe and the billions and billions of planets, there may only be just one planet uniquely designed to allow life to exist. That one planet is Earth. This extreme fine-tuning of our physical world, exactly correct right from the immediate start to enable life, points to the existence of an intelligent designer. An intelligent designer suggests the existence of a creator, God.

Again, not only does the Bible get the beginning of the universe correct, but it also correctly identifies how earth and its various ecosystems necessary for life came to be and in the correct chronological order. It also clearly identifies an intelligent designer, God, who is responsible for setting all the dials in earth's biosphere on a precise razor's edge necessary for life to exist. The account and explanation of these matters given by the Bible exactly matches what modern science is stating. Coincidence?

Chapter 3

How Did Life Begin?

860 to 250 Million Years BC: Bible Days 5-6

Both my father and mother came from small family farms in northeast Iowa. Once they were married, my dad worked at the local meat-packing plant to support our family. Although our needs were met, when I decided to enroll in engineering, it was on a prayer, knowing I had to be financially self-sufficient. Even though I worked multiple jobs while in high school, including commercial fishing with my father on the Mississippi River, and had saved for college from a very young age, I simply didn't have enough to pay for the engineering education I dreamed about. Not even close. I figured by working at the university's food service between classes, and by picking up a summer job after my freshman year, I had just enough to get me through my sophomore year if there were no unexpected expenditures. At that point I would be flat broke, and my dreams would fade fast without the funding to continue.

To pay for my education and complete my degree, I needed a lucky break. I needed some form of outside intervention to help me get started in life. I really needed God's help. As I said, I went to college on a prayer. Little did I know God would answer that prayer in a big way. Toward the end of my sophomore year, I learned the university I was attending was one of the few engineering schools selected by General Motors for potential scholarships. They offered full-ride scholarships to the selected recipients through a national competitive selection process. Long story short, I received one of these coveted scholarships, and the rest is history. To this day I am extremely grateful to General Motors for providing me this start in my engineering life. Without it, my dream of becoming an engineer may have never been realized.

Life and living organisms are much like this. With all our medical sophistication and technical know-how, science still does not know how to create life from nonlife. How do you take nonliving atoms and molecules, clump them together, and create a living thing? It is beyond human understanding. Life simply cannot spring into being on its own from innate atoms and molecules. Just like funding my engineering education, life on earth required intervention from an outside source to come into being. All the various life forms on earth came into existence through the miraculous, creative hand of God.

By the conclusion of day 4, the earth is a perfect biosphere for supporting life. Located in the safe mid-zone of a spiral galaxy, surrounded by larger planets to take the blow on stray asteroids, and with a circular orbit to have uniform temperature. It has a stable sun of just the right size and just the right distance away so the temperatures are within a life-permitting band. It also has a moon to keep its tilt stable for consistent seasons and to create tides for circulating the oceans to moderate temperatures. Last, but certainly not least, the earth has liquid water on its surface necessary for life and lush plants and vegetation to produce oxygen necessary for life. With the stage set for animal life to appear, right on cue animal life appears on the scene.

860 Million Years Ago: Day 5

> And God said, "Let the water teem with living creatures, and let birds fly above the earth across the expanse of the sky." So God created the great creatures of the sea and every living and moving thing with which the water teems, according to their kinds, and every winged bird according to its kind.

> And God saw that it was good. God blessed them and said, "Be fruitful and increase in number and fill the water of the seas, and let the birds increase on the earth." And there was evening, and there was morning—the fifth day. (Genesis 1:20–23)

The Bible states there was a sudden appearance of animal life with no mention or hint of slow evolutionary processes taking place over millions of years. Interesting. So what is science's explanation for how to get living organisms out of nonliving molecules and atoms? In short, to this day there is no scientific explanation of how to take nonliving matter and create living matter out of it. Scientifically speaking, life is a miracle. Creation of life from nonlife is beyond human understanding and explanation.

In 1953, Stanley Miller, a graduate student at the University of Chicago, conducted an experiment that captured much attention.[1] He put an electric charge through a mixture of methane, ammonia, hydrogen gas, and water vapor to simulate lightning going through the atmosphere of a young earth. After a couple of days, a goo appeared in the reaction vessel identified as amino acids. Since amino acids are the building blocks of proteins, and proteins in turn are an essential part of living organisms, could it be he found a way to create life from nonlife? But as it turned out, the amino acids did not develop into anything else; they just remained goo in the vessel over time.

Nobody knows for sure the exact composition of the early atmosphere, but there is no evidence for a methane-ammonia atmosphere on earth as used by Miller in his experiment. Current consensus is it was probably carbon dioxide, nitrogen, and water vapor. If you repeat his experiment with these components you get formaldehyde.[2] Formaldehyde is a poisonous toxin used to embalm dead bodies and is hardly conducive to life.

Nonetheless, is it possible to create a living cell from amino acids like the kind Miller created? Doug Axe, an accomplished and well-respected molecular biologist studied the possibility of creating a protein chain roll by a random, unguided arrangement of amino acids. He considered a protein consisting of 150 amino acids and found the odds to be 1 in 10^{74}.[3] To put that into perspective, there are only an estimated 10^{68-72} atoms in the entire universe.[4] It would take all the atoms in one hundred to one million universes to equal this number, 10^{74}. The odds of a random, unguided arrangement of amino acids forming into a protein roll needed for life would be virtually zero. Nonexistent. Further, this still would not be a life form. This would just be a protein roll. There would be a plethora of other similar complex structures and organisms that would have to come together exactly right at the same time to even possibly create a living cell. So random, unguided mutations cannot possibly create a new protein fold and have an even lower chance of creating a new life form.

Since there really is not a scientific explanation for the origin of life, let's examine what Charles Darwin put forth in his renowned book *The Origin of Species*. Charles Darwin formed the basis of his theory of evolution due to his travels to the Galapagos Islands in the Pacific Ocean off the coast of Ecuador. There he observed many species of finches that seemed all related, and this formed the basis of the theory of evolution he would later develop.

Figure 3.1: Charles Darwin

Charles Darwin's theory proposed there is a tree of life where all living species could ultimately trace their roots to a common ancestor. The base of the tree of life would be a single-celled organism. Due to random mutations, natural variation, and natural selection, over time these organisms would develop into slightly more complex life forms. This process would continue over millions of years and with millions of organisms. In a sense it was like millions of "experiments" where nature would decide what variations would survive and which would die off. These "experiments" would continually be taking place, and after millions of years, organisms as complex as humans would emerge.

Darwinian evolution can be thought of by observing the long neck of a giraffe. Giraffes feed by eating tree leaves. Suppose giraffes started off in life with neck lengths like a horse. When leaves became scarce during say drought periods, the giraffes with slightly longer necks would be better adapted to survive since they could reach higher in the tree to eat. Over a long period of time, longer- and longer-necked giraffes would have been favored for survival by nature. This is how evolution would explain the development of the long neck of the giraffe. It is nature's way of selecting the most-fit species among the naturally occurring variation within the species. Never mind that the theory does not explain how the extra vertebrates in the giraffe's neck magically appear.

In his book, Darwin devoted a chapter to *Difficulties of the Theory* where he discusses and admits the shortcomings of his theory to cover various items. In his own words, "But, as by this theory innumerable transitional forms must have existed, why do we not find them embedded in countless numbers in the crust of the earth?"[5] Further, "To suppose that the eye with all its inimitable contrivances for adjusting the focus to different distances, for admitting different amounts of light, and for the correction of spherical and chromatic aberration, could have been formed by natural selection, seems, I freely confess, absurd in the highest degree."[6] Still further, he raises the point that if you find evidence of sudden appearance (saltation) in the fossil record, this would be evidence of special creation, which is to say a creator. Darwin's hunches were right in all three of these areas. Scientific data over roughly the last two hundred years since he made these statements has proven the shortcomings of his theory of evolution.

So what has science found during this time span? Instead of a fossil record gradually increasing in diversity and number of species, there was a biological big bang like the big bang for the universe itself. It is called the Cambrian Explosion and occurred over 500 million years ago.[7] These are the very first creatures of the sea the Bible mentions. During the Cambrian period, there was a sudden explosion of life that cannot be predicted or explained by evolutionary processes. From a geological dating perspective, it happened virtually overnight. There was nothing for billions of years, and then suddenly and dramatically, most of the life forms appear all at once. These new blueprints for the various animal phyla included such things as compound eyes, articulated limbs, spinal cords, and skeletal structures.

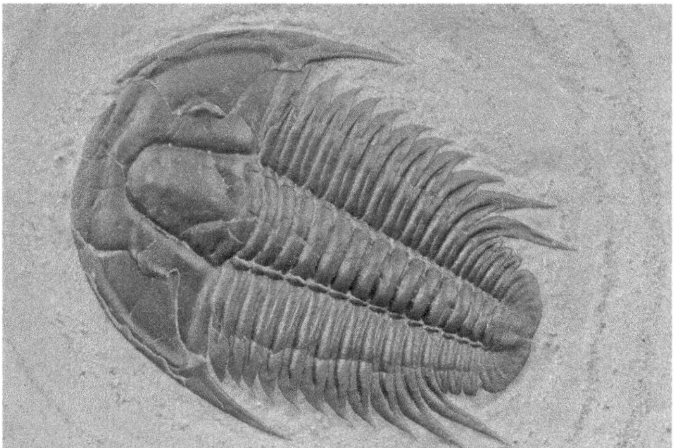

Figure 3.2: Trilobite fossil from Cambrian Explosion

The Cambrian Explosion has been observed around the world,

with fossil remains on all seven continents. Darwin himself observed fossils from the Cambrian Explosion in Wales. His reaction to this evidence was that he thought the fossil record was incomplete. The prevalent thought at this time was the answers laid at the bottom of the ocean. However, with the advent of oil companies drilling at the bottom of the ocean floor in search of oil, researchers have scoured through the drill plugs brought up. Some fossils have been found, but no new types of organisms have been found, and none of them predate the Cambrian period.

Since the 1960s scientists have used radioactive minerals to date underwater sediments and have created a digital map of the earth's age. The rocks in the ocean are hundreds of millions of years younger than the Cambrian period. Therefore, the ocean floors do not contain pre-Cambrian fossils. As a result, the consensus is the fossil record is mostly complete.

Still another thought was the animal life forms prior to the Cambrian period were too soft to be fossilized. In 1984 this thought was countered by one of the most important finds of the history of paleontology discovered in Yunnan, China.[8] Just beneath the Cambrian fossils, and therefore just prior chronologically, are excellently preserved soft-bodied animals, eggs, and embryos from life forms present in the Cambrian period, but no transitional species. If this site can preserve something as soft as an embryo, why could it not preserve the transitional link to the hard-shelled trilobites, if such a species existed? The answer is simply there are no transitional species. Again, further evidence the fossil record is mostly complete.

If Darwinian evolution were true, we would expect to see a gradual increase in the number of basic animal body plans stretching out over long periods of times. What we actually see in the fossil record is only single-celled organisms on the earth for four billion years. Then suddenly and dramatically, as if overnight, most of the life forms on earth appear. The period is so short scientist cannot discern it. Per Darwin himself, if scientific evidence of saltation (sudden appearance) was found, he wrote this would be strong evidence of special creation, God. This is exactly what the fossil record shows.

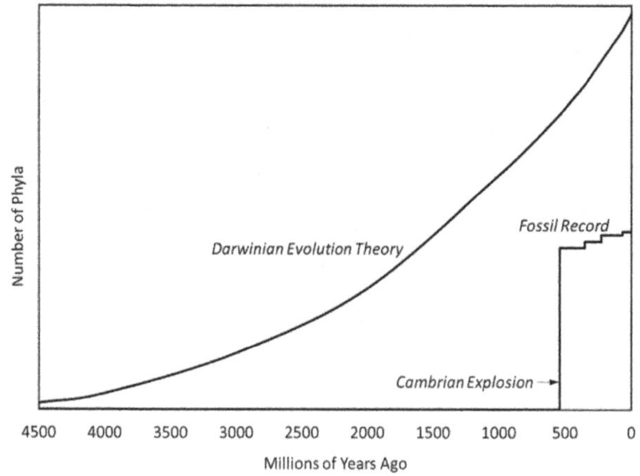

Figure 3.3: Darwinian evolution versus fossil record

Our current scientific understanding of the chronological rollout of life during this period goes something like this:[9]

No multicelled life forms on earth	4500–580 MYA
Cambrian Explosion—most modern phyla of animals appear	580–550 MYA
Comb jellies, sponges, corals, and sea anemones appear	550 MYA
Major diversification of living things in the ocean: chordates, arthropods, etc.	535 MYA
First vertebrates with true bones (jawless fish)	485 MYA
Vegetation and seed-bearing plants	363 MYA
Large sharks, ratfishes, and hagfish	350 MYA
Diversification of amphibians	340 MYA

Note: MYA = millions of years ago

Figure 3.4: Artist rendition of Cambrian Explosion life forms

250 Million Years Ago: Day 6

Let's move on in time to what the Bible describes in day 6:

> And God said, "Let the land produce living creatures according to their kinds: livestock, creatures that move along the ground, and wild animals, each according to its kind." And it was so. God made the wild animals according to their kinds, the livestock according to their kinds, and all the creatures that move along the ground according to their kinds. And God saw that it was good. Then God said, "Let us make man in our image, in our likeness, and let them rule over the fish of the sea and the birds of the air, over the livestock, over all the earth, and over all the creatures that move along the ground." So God created man in his own image, in the image of God he created him; male and female he created them. God blessed them and said to them, "Be fruitful and increase in number; fill the earth and subdue it. Rule over the fish of the sea and the birds of the air and over every living creature that moves on the ground." Then God said, "I give you

> every seed-bearing plant on the face of the whole earth and every tree that has fruit with seed in it. They will be yours for food. And to all the beasts of the earth and all the birds of the air and all the creatures that move on the ground—everything that has the breath of life in it—I give every green plant for food." And it was so. God saw all that he had made, and it was very good. And there was evening, and there was morning—the sixth day. (Genesis 1:24–31)

Continuing in the chronological rollout of living animals and creatures on earth:[10]

Earliest dinosaurs	225 MYA
First members of the Stegosauri group of dinosaurs	176 MYA
Earliest salamanders, newts, cryptoclidids, elasmosaurid plesiosaurs, etc., mammals	170 MYA
First blood-sucking insects	155 MYA
Earliest bees	100 MYA
Snakes and nuculanid bivalves	90 MYA
Tyrannosaurus and triceratops dinosaurs	68 MYA
Extinction event eradicates half of all animal species and all dinosaurs except birds	66 MYA
Modern bird groups diversify	63 MYA
First deer	25 MYA
First giraffes, hyenas, bears, and giant anteaters, increase in bird diversity	20 MYA

Figure 3.5: Artist rendering of Tyrannosaurus rex

If you take the time to read through and study the table above, you will note dinosaurs first appeared around 225 million years ago and then became extinct around 66 million years ago. If you are familiar with the Bible, did you ever wonder why the Bible does not explicitly mention dinosaurs? First, not all created animals are mentioned in the Bible. As was previously stated, although the Bible contains a lot of science and history, it is not a science or history book. However, with something as big and imposing as a dinosaur, you would think the Bible would mention them. Some have looked at the following passage in the book of Job and concluded the original Hebrew word translated into the English word *behemoth* could mean dinosaur:

> Look at the behemoth, which I made along with you and which feeds on grass like an ox. What strength he has in his loins, what power in the muscles of his belly! His tail sways like a cedar; the sinews of his thighs are close-knit. His bones are tubed of bronze, his limbs like rods of iron. He ranks first among the works of God, yet his Maker can approach him with his sword. (Job 40:15–19)

The only other passage that could possibly imply a dinosaur comes from the next chapter, Job 41, where the word *leviathan* is used:

> Can you pull in the leviathan with a fishhook or tie down his tongue with a rope? Can you put a cord through his nose or pierce his jaw with a hook? Will he keep begging you with gentle words? Will he make an agreement with you for you to take him as your slave for life? Can you make a pet of him like a bird or put him on a leash for your girls? (Job 41:1–5)

Bible commentaries have suggested the passage from Job 40 was possibly referring to the hippopotamus or the elephant and the passage in Job 41 to the crocodile. There is no scientific evidence to indicate dinosaurs and humans coexisted. Dinosaurs came and went and then millions of years later—66 million, in fact—humans appeared. So, why did the Bible writers not mention dinosaurs? Because they had no knowledge or even inclination such animals ever existed. The first dinosaur bones were found in 1819, which means humankind only knew about dinosaurs starting only two hundred years ago, and the Bible was written well before then.[11]

So how can life be accounted for apart from creation? Again, considering Darwinian evolution, it can be stated there are no transitional forms between the major divisions of life. In other words, fish remain fish, amphibians remain amphibians, reptiles remain reptiles, birds remain birds, mammals remain mammals, and humans remain humans. There simply are no transitional species. None. Of the millions of fossil remains that have been dug up, not one transitional life form has ever been found. Not one! If Darwinian evolution is true, the fossil records should be littered with transitional species, and they should be present today. The bottom line is Darwinian evolution is not happening now, and it has not happened in the past. It is a theory that has been proven wrong decisively, from the smallest of living organism to the most complex.

If we think back to our giraffe example, if Darwinian evolution were true, we would expect to see giraffes of progressively longer necks in the fossil record. What is actually seen in the fossil record is no evidence of evolution of the giraffe. There are no species of giraffes with progressively longer and longer necks. We either find a giraffe as it appears today, or we find nothing. There is no evidence in the fossil record of this macroevolution taking place. The same can be said of all other living species.

Darwinian evolution or macroevolution states that you start at the species level. Then due to random mutation, random variation, and natural selection, small differences in the species lead to new genera. Over time these new genera further lead to new families, then new orders, new classes, and finally new phyla, or body plans. A progression from little differences between species leading into big changes. But this theory just simply does not hold in light of scientific data and observation.

So how does nature progress? Consider the automobile. The basic body plan has been around for a long time: engine, drive train, four wheels, body, and controls. Over time the various components and subcomponents have evolved, but the basic body plan remains intact. A modern car, although much more refined than Henry Ford's first car, greatly resembles the original basic body plan. This top-down fashion is how life forms are observed to change over time. It is called microevolution. The big differences via the phyla appear first, and then over time smaller differences lead to new classes, then orders, and families, genera, and finally species under each original phyla. Natural, random processes take an existing phyla or body plan, and then through natural selection, or survival of the fittest, allow that body plan to be refined for its environment. This occurs through variations that already exist within the DNA of that given basic body plan, such as brown eyes versus blue, or long beaks versus short beaks. It's a relatively minor variation on a given body plan. Conversely, nature cannot take an existing body plan and then through random variation and natural selection add new components or complexity to the system, such as adding more vertebrates to a giraffe's neck to lengthen it.

Consider the human design process again. Complex engineering structures, such as a fighter jet or a suspension bridge, are designed in a top-down manner; high-level systems are designed first, and then lower level subsystems are designed next, on down to detailed level design for all the components. Engineers do not start with a bucket of bolts, angle iron, and welding rods and just start assembling and building and then viola, a year later a suspension bridge appears. In fact, complex designs coming about by bringing together many subsystems can occur only with the guidance of intelligence. Complex designs and structures are a tell-tale sign of an intelligent designer.

The assembly of matter, life, and the whole universe we live in could not be explained through naturalistic causes. Michael Behe, a professor of biochemistry at Lehigh University, said it best when he stated there are no feasible evolutionary explanation for some "irreducibly complex systems"—even in the simplest cells and molecular systems.[12] Think of a mousetrap representing a very simplistic example of one of these systems. It consists of a base plate, coil spring, hammer, catch, trigger, and associated staples to hold the various components to the base plate. Even if we could envision a way these individual components could be generated by evolutionary processes, we would still be faced with the daunting puzzle of how did the components get attached and assembled to the base plate? Even more daunting, how did the mousetrap get set? To set the mousetrap, the hammer had to be cocked back against the spring, the trigger had to be placed to hold the hammer back, and then the trigger had to be carefully and correctly inserted into the catch. If you have ever set a mousetrap, you know that even then there are no guarantees it will stay set once you release it. In fact, it may take several attempts to set it. Well this same scenario plays out with real-world life systems. Numerous "irreducibly complex systems" that cannot be explained by unguided, random evolutionary processes and their appearance strongly indicates the influence of an intelligent designer—a designer who can not only design and bring about the mousetrap but who can also set it. In days 2, 3, and 4 we considered a few examples pointing to an intelligent designer as they relate to the physical, nonliving world. Now let's consider a few examples from the living world pointing to an intelligent designer.

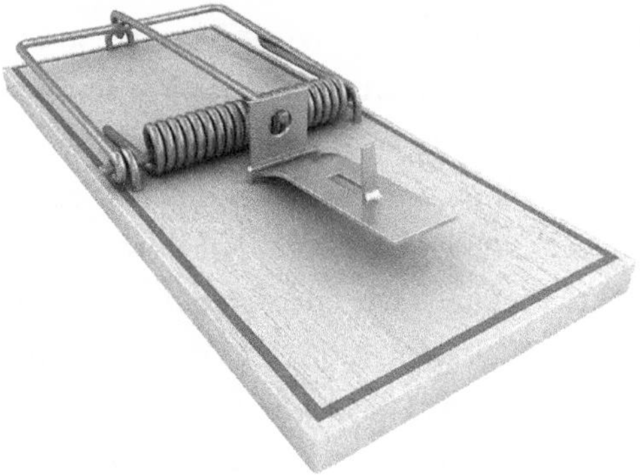

Figure 3.6: Mousetrap

First, consider biochemistry and the cell, which is the smallest living unit. The cell is like a very complex living factory with 10^{12}, or a thousand billion atoms in a typical cell. The cell as Darwin knew it consisted of a nucleolus, a nucleus, and a cell membrane. Essentially to Darwin the cell was like a chicken egg with a center yolk-like nucleus, surrounded by a white-like nucleolus, all incased in a shell-like membrane. Darwin would probably be astonished if he knew the much greater complexity existing in the cell and researchers are still exploring and learning more to this day. The typical cell as its now known consists of a: 1) nucleolus, 2) nucleus, 3) ribosome, 4) vesicle, 5) rough endoplasmic reticulum, 6) golgi apparatus, 7) cytoskeleton, 8) smooth endoplasmic reticulum, 9) mitochondrion, 10) vacuole, 11) cytosol, 12) lysosome, 13) centrosome, and 14) cell membrane. And each of the fourteen components are of much higher complexity than ever imagined. Further, each of these fourteen components within the cell are interdependent and beg the question, how could they have arrived exactly at the same time and arranged themselves perfectly within the cell simultaneously to enable life?

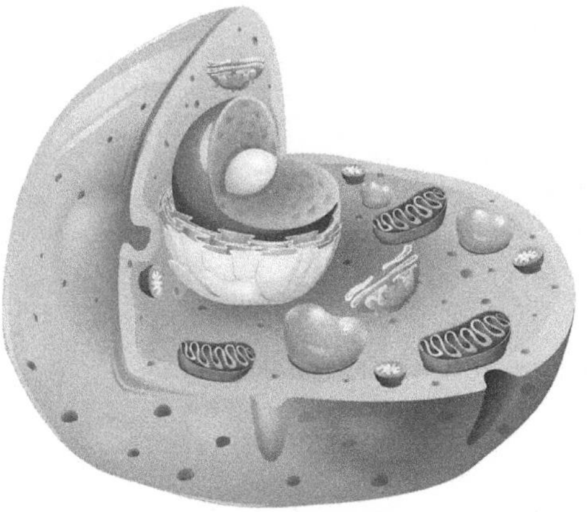

Figure 3.7: Artist rendering of the human cell

As a good example of a "mousetrap" cell, consider the bacteria cell. The cell has a flagellum that looks like a mouse tail coming out of the cell. It behaves like a rotary propeller to move the bacterial cell. Proteins act as bushings to allow the drive shaft to penetrate the cell wall and attach to the internal rotary motor. It is energized by the flow of acid through the bacterial membrane. The flagellum propeller can spin at 10,000 RPM. It can stop within a quarter turn and instantly spin the other way 10,000 RPM.[13] To put that in perspective, a car engine rotates roughly in the 2000–2500 RPM range on the highway. The astonishing propeller mechanism and rotary motor inside the cell begs the question, "Who set this mousetrap?" How could this be arrived at through undirected, random evolutionary forces? Like a set mousetrap, all of the elements had to come together at exactly the same time for the cell to be a living, functional entity. It strongly points toward an intelligent designer.

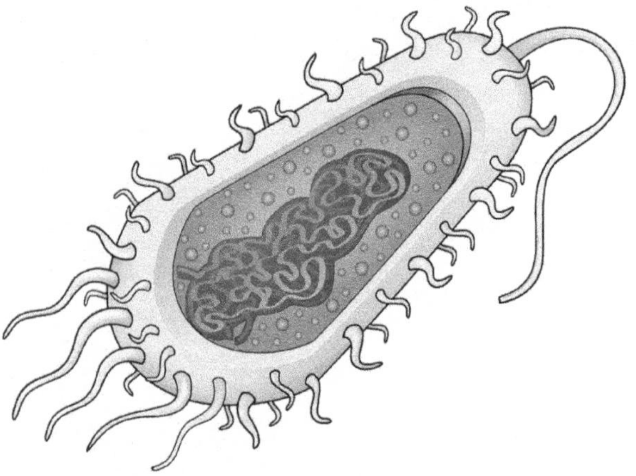

Figure 3.8: Bacterial flagellum

Now consider deoxyribonucleic acid, or DNA, which is located within the cell itself. DNA was first discovered in 1953 by James Watson and Francis Crick, almost one hundred years after Charles Darwin and his theory of evolution appeared.[14] DNA is a molecule that resides within the living cells of all organisms and carries the genetic information or instructions for the organism on how to live and operate. The information stored in just one tiny strand of DNA is immense. It is the instruction manual for the organism. The information is stored via four chemical bases: adenine (A), guanine (G), cytosine (C), and thymine (T). The base chemicals always pair up such that A and T are always together, and C and G are always together. The DNA strand looks like a very long, spiraling ladder. Each rung of the DNA ladder contains two pairs of the DNA bases, A/T and G/C. The sides of the DNA ladder are sugar and phosphate molecules. If stretched out, each DNA strand would be around six feet long, and all the DNA in one person put together would be about twice the diameter of the solar system.[15] The DNA is tightly twisted and becomes packaged as a chromosome.

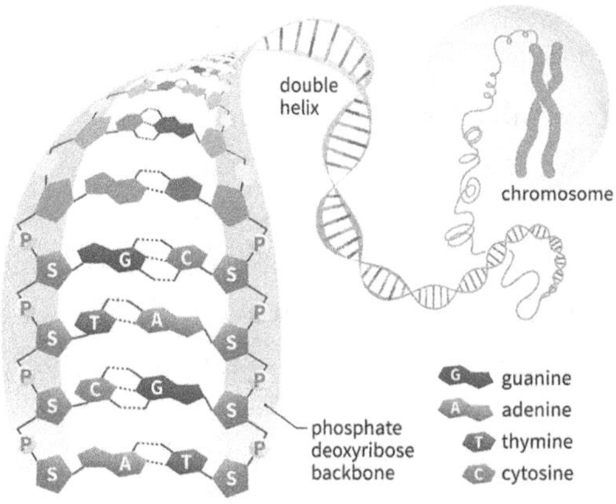

Figure 3.9: DNA packaged as chromosome

The likeness between DNA coding and a modern digital computer is stunning. The computer coding system is based on a binary system of ones and zeros. A row of computer memory might read something like: 1101100100101001. DNA coding is based on four chemicals that compose each "rung" on the "DNA ladder." Collectively the coding information might read something like: GCTACGATTACGGCAT. The eerie similarity between the two information storage systems suggests just as an intelligent designer is responsible for the computer storage system, there is an intelligent designer responsible for DNA. Further, the density of information stored in DNA is staggering compared to a computer storage system.

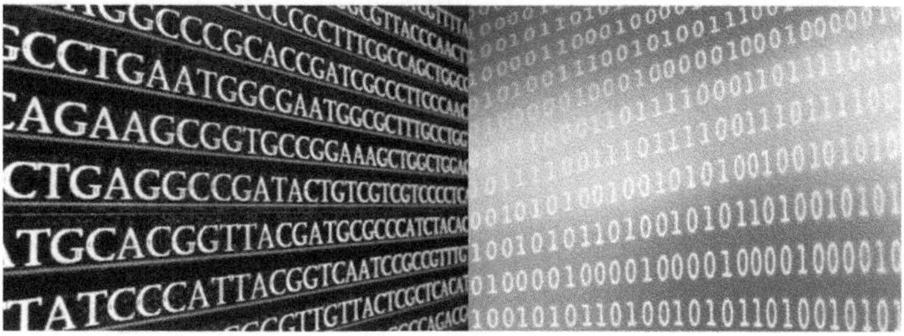

Figure 3.10: DNA vs. computer information storage

Next, consider the protein structure. The protein roll-up structures in a cell are like very complicated Rubik's cubes. Amino acids are first assembled precisely in fixed order into lengths of chains. These chains then combine to form a secondary structure. Think of them as ribbon-like structures. Then these ribbons, of differing size and shape are precisely rolled up into tertiary structures. Think of them as a ball of ribbons that cannot be simply wadded up and compressed together, but more like multifaceted Rubik's cubes that can only fit together in one fashion. Then these tertiary structures are combined with various other tertiary structures to form a quaternary structure. Each component must fit exactly and precisely together in this interwoven complex. Fred Hoyle and colleague Chandra Wichramasinghe calculated the odds that all the functional proteins necessary for life might form in one place by random events is 1 X 10^{40000}![16] Virtually unimaginable odds. Realizing this and its implications, Fred Hoyle stated,

> Life could not have originated here on the earth. Nor does it look as though biological evolution can be explained from within an earthbound theory of life. Genes from outside the earth are needed to drive the evolutionary process. This much can be consolidated by strictly scientific means, by experiment, observations and calculation.[17]

Keep in mind, Hoyle was an atheist. What he was basically saying is functional, life-enabling proteins are too complex to have originated by evolutionary processes. Life had to originate from a creative force outside of the earth.

Nobel laureate Francis Crick (who discovered the DNA code mentioned above) has concluded, like Hoyle and others, life could not have originated here on earth by any natural process. However, because of their atheistic beliefs, they have been turned to the panspermia hypothesis: Life's genetic material was sent here from somewhere else! In reality, however, this only kicks the can down the cosmic alley. All the arguments for an intelligent designer remain intact, and it only moves to a new planet. Further, it is opposed to all the evidence previously examined, indicating it is highly unlikely there is another place within our universe beyond the earth that can support life.

So what does all of this evidence for the origin of life suggest? First, the chronological rollout of life forms in the Bible is supported by the fossil record left behind. Again, writing thousands of years ago, how did Moses get it right without some form of divine guidance? Second, scientifically speaking, the creation of life is a miracle. Modern science and medicine cannot create a single strand of DNA that contains the building block blueprint for living organisms. How life began is a scientific miracle. Third, Darwinian macroevolution is not scientifically supported. The building blocks of life, such as DNA, are too complex to arrive at through evolutionary means. To have an eye, for instance, requires all the elements present together at the same time initially. It cannot be arrived at through naturalistic, evolutionary processes. Fourth, life began suddenly on earth, not gradually. The big bang of living things was the Cambrian Explosion. It occurred in virtually a geological instant. It occurred in much less time than scientists can discern the geological time difference. Evolutionary processes would take millions, if not billions, of years to occur. The Cambrian Explosion, when most animal life forms came about, occurred in an instant. Fifth, the design of life forms takes intelligence. It takes an extremely intelligent designer, much beyond human capability, to design life. Taken collectively, what does this indicate? It suggests life was created by an extremely intelligent designer.

The creation of life by an extremely intelligent designer outside of the earth, and the chronological rollout of the various life forms given in the Bible, exactly matches modern scientific thought. Coincidence?

Chapter 4

Are We Physically Evolved Apes?

250 Million Years to 4000 BC: Bible Day 6

Several times throughout my engineering career, I have been called into legal duty as an engineering expert witness. It was my job to closely examine the evidence of a given case and then, under oath during examination, weigh in with my knowledge and experience regarding the technical aspects of the case. One case I was involved in concerned a claimed electrical problem with a component. The plaintiff's technical expert asserted there was an electrical short in a particular component, leading to further problems and financial loss for the plaintiff. After examination of the evidence of the complete system, he pointed his finger at this component and testified if a fusible link had been installed in the power lead going into the component, the plaintiff's loss would have been avoided. He concluded since such fuse was nonexistent, the manufacturer of the component was responsible for the plaintiff's financial loss.

When I was brought into the case, I asked to examine the evidence and the various components directly myself. The first item of business performed was to x-ray the power lead attached to the component. When this was done, the case almost became laughable.

Clearly, the plaintiff's technical expert knew nothing about fusible links, such as was built into this power lead. He jumped to the conclusion that there was no fuse present that would have prevented electrical problems since he could not see any external fuse in the system. A fusible link, however, is built right into the wiring itself and is not readily apparent from a casual glance at the insulated wire. A fusible link consists of a section of wiring significantly smaller in cross-sectional area than the main wire and is electrically connected in series with the main wire. When the insulation is put over the wire, the external appearance of the wire looks uniform throughout the wire even though the fusible link section is much different inside. If an over current condition occurs, due to its smaller cross-section, the fusible link heats up quickly and then melts, which causes a discontinuity in the wire. With a discontinuity, or open in the wire, current can no longer flow, and further problems are prevented. When the power lead was put into the x-ray machine, the fusible link could clearly be seen in the wire in its pristine state, with no evidence of an over current condition. This was clear evidence the alleged component was not the root cause of the plaintiff's problem. The plaintiff's expert witness clearly lacked a basic understanding of fusible links and jumped to the wrong conclusion.

This same lack of basic understanding is prevalent among those who assert humans descended from apes and chimps. We have all seen the progressive drawings showing how knuckle-walking apes evolve slowly over time to stand upright and grow in height to become an upright, walking human. This too involves a link, but this time, the link is truly missing! The half-human, half-ape creatures shown in the middle are a figment of an artist's imagination. They have never existed, and there is no proof or evidence they ever did. When one critically examines the evidence, as we will do in this chapter, the theory of evolution falls apart. The evidence is simply not there. There is, however, solid scientific evidence humankind was created exactly as the Bible indicates. The Bible proclaims the creation of all living things culminated, and ended, with the creation of humankind. In fact, per the fossil record and archeology, humans are indeed the last species to appear on planet earth. On this fact, the Bible account written thirty-five hundred years ago gets a perfect score again. Another coincidence?

We have previously looked at many of the fallacies of evolution. The Cambrian Explosion, when most of the phyla of all animal forms suddenly burst on the scene, debunks the theory of evolution. Life forms did not slowly evolve over time over millions of years as required by naturalistic evolutionary processes. Life appeared suddenly in a geological instant, as witnessed by the fossil records. For billions of years there was only single-celled bacteria, and then in an instant, there appeared most of the body forms (phyla) of all animals. This undisputed, worldwide scientific evidence dispels the notion life forms were created through evolutionary processes. Even the simplest of life forms, single-celled bacteria, is a mystery to science. With all our modern sophistication and medical technology, we still don't know how to create life. It takes existing created life to reproduce life. We cannot take lifeless matter and create life. We also looked at the complexity of the building blocks of life itself, such as the cell and DNA within the cell, or subsystems such as the eye, and saw again there was no building block approach to these designs that could be arrived at through an unguided, natural evolutionary process. The summation of the scientific information points to some form of an intelligent creator responsible for the creation of life, and this points to God.

But despite all this factual evidence, is it possible somehow, some way humans evolved from a common ancestor as apes? After all, when you look at humans and apes or chimpanzees, it's undeniable we share a lot of similar-looking body parts. Turning aside all the evidence against macroevolution of a chimp and human sharing a common ancestor millions of years ago, could it be true? Let's examine it in greater detail with the benefit of all our modern scientific and medical discoveries.

We will pick up the trail chronologically where we last stopped and follow the appearance of primates. We will briefly highlight some of the species identified by evolutionists that they claim led to human beings, and then we will do a much deeper dive on this subject.

Primates are an order within mammals characterized by warm-blooded vertebras, with a coat of hair, five digits on hands and feet, and a large brain size to body size ratio. Primates are the most developed and intelligent group of mammals and include monkeys, apes, and humans. Per evolutionists, modern humans, or Homo sapiens, are the last of a long line of primates that evolved from a common ancestor starting with the gibbon, then orangutan, then gorilla, then chimp, and then human.[1]

50–55 Million Years Ago: Day 6—First Primates Appear

The first primates appeared around 50 to 55 million years ago, with their fossil remains being found in North America, Europe, and Asia. They were squirrel-like in both size and appearance. They had hands and feet that were adept for climbing trees where they dwelt.

15 Million Years Ago: Day 6—Great Apes Appear

The great apes, hominidae, appear for the first time around 15 million years ago. Current animals under the great ape classification would include chimpanzees, bonobos, gorillas, orangutans, and humans. The great apes are characterized as being large, tailless primates.

3.2 Million Years Ago: Day 6—Australopithecus Afarensis Appear

Another species in the supposed evolutionary path to humans was Australopithecus afarensis, which lived between 3.9 and 2.9 million years ago. The celebrated "Lucy" fossil remains are an early Australopithecus afarensis specimen and dates to around 3.2 million years ago. Roughly 40 percent of the skeleton was found in Ethiopia in 1974 by Dr. Donald Johansson.[2]

1.8 Million Years Ago: Day 6—Homo Erectus Appear

The first skeleton remains of Homo erectus were found by a team led by Dutch anatomist Eugen Dubois in 1891 on the island of

Java in modern-day Indonesia. A large skull-cap, later three teeth, and a year later, a thigh bone were found in the area. Inspired by Darwin's work, Dubois claimed it was the "missing link" between apes and humans. Later Dubois's claim and discovery were found to be a hoax.[3] The bones were not from a single, new species but rather multiple different, already identified species.

250,000 Years Ago: Day 6—Neanderthal Appear

Neanderthal lived during the last ice age and lived in caves for survival. Consequently they have come to be known as cave men, and the cartoon caricatures come to mind for many people. Fossil remains of what is now known as Neanderthal man were first discovered in 1856 in Germany's Neander Valley.[4] Fossil remains have been identified as Neanderthal have been found throughout Europe, Western Asia, and the Middle East. Neanderthals were the first known human-like species to walk upright. Researchers are arriving at the conclusion that physically, Neanderthals were the same as modern humans. As a species, they became extinct around forty thousand years ago, but the exact reason is still unknown.

40,000 Years Ago: Day 6—Cro-Magnon Appear

Cro-Magnon man fossil remains were first found in the Cro-Magnon cave of Dordogne, France, in 1868.[5] For years, Cro-Magnon man was identified as a separate species from humans. But recent DNA studies and investigations have revealed this species is also physically the same as modern humans. Consequently, Cro-Magnon is no longer listed as a separate species but known as early Homo sapiens.

40,000 Years Ago: Day 6—Denisovan Appear

In 2010 in the remote Denisova Cave in the Altai Mountains in Siberia, scientists discovered a single finger bone fragment of a juvenile female who lived forty-one thousand years ago.[6] To date only this pinkie finger bone and three teeth have been found of this whole classification of species known as Denisova hominin.

So when did we, modern humans, first appear? Let's turn to the Bible for an answer.

6000 Years Ago: Day 6

> Then God said, "Let us make man in our image, in our likeness, and let them rule over the fish of the sea and the birds of the air, over the livestock, over all the earth, and over all the creatures that move along the ground." So God created man in his own image, in the image of God he created him; male and female he created them. God blessed them and said to them, "Be fruitful and increase in number; fill the earth and subdue it. Rule over the fish of the sea and the birds of the air and over every living creature that moves on the ground." Then God said, "I give you every seed-bearing plant on the face of the whole earth and every tree that has fruit with seed in it. They will be yours for food. And to all the beasts of the earth and all the birds of the air and all the creatures that move on the ground—everything that has the breath of life in it—I give every green plant for food." And it was so. God saw all that he had made, and it was very good. And there was evening, and there was morning—the sixth day. (Genesis 1:26–31)

Although you will not see it in the mainstream news, the latest scientific human genome DNA studies indicate modern humans appeared on the earth for the first time around six thousand years ago, in complete agreement with the Bible. This finding is the result of hundreds of worldwide researchers and billions of dollars. Although the Bible has been steadfast in its account from the day each word was written, humankind's scientific investigation into the world around him has drawn closer and closer to the biblical timing for the appearance of humans as around six thousand years ago. In the last fifteen years, with the conclusion of the Human Genome Project and spinoff projects, science has been in agreement with what the Bible has been saying all along: humankind first appeared six thousand years ago, as we will see below.

As mentioned earlier, we have all seen the evolutionary sketches depicting chimps on the left side, and after a series of intermediate ape-like forms, evolving into humans. Factually speaking, these cartoons are fictional. The multitude of intermediate ape-like forms in the middle simply do not exist, have never been found, and are not supported by any scientific studies. Gibbon apes appear in the fossil record and still exist. Gorillas appear in the fossil record and still exist. Chimps appear in the fossil record and still exist. Humans appear in the fossil record and still exist. The multitude of transitional species that evolution requires to fill in the gaps in the middle of these evolutionary sketches simply do not exist in the fossil record.

For starters, let's examine just one facet of this transition missing from the fossil record: the transition to walking upright. Gibbons, gorillas, and chimps are all knuckle walkers. Although they can walk upright for periods of time, their main mode of walking is on all fours, utilizing the knuckles on their front legs. Humans, on the other hand, walk upright on two legs. This is called bipedalism. If evolution were true, we would expect to see transitional species that evolved over lengthy periods of time from knuckle walkers into bipedalism. We don't. We have knuckle walkers and we have bipedal humans in the fossil record. Nothing in between.

So how big is this gap? Anatomically speaking, huge. For an ape or chimp to evolve into an upright walking species, according to Dr. Fazale Rana in his article "The Leap to Two Feet: The Sudden Appearance of Bipedalism," the following anatomical changes would have to occur:[7]

1. Relocation of the spinal cord opening in the skull to accommodate the new head position.

2. Restructuring of the inner ear bones integral for balance suitable for bipedalism.
3. Introduction of curvature in the spine to provide spring movement allowing bipedalism.
4. Restructuring of the rib cage shape to allow use of the arms for nonwalking functions.
5. Reshaping the pelvis to be lower and broader for necessary hip joints and muscles.
6. Longer lower limbs and a change in the angle the femur makes with the body.
7. Enlarged joint surfaces in the legs to accommodate the higher weight carried.
8. Extensive changes to the musculature system to accommodate the upright position.

Transitional species representing the slow change over time necessary for evolutionary forces to have been responsible for the appearance of bipedalism simply do not exist in the fossil record. The anatomical chasm between species is huge. We have knuckle-walking gorillas and chimps, and we have upright humans with nothing in between. The fossil record does not support evolutionary theory claiming gorillas, chimps, and humans share a common ancestor. If humans evolved from chimps, then the fossil record would be littered with transitional species and we should see transitional species today. The evidence clearly does not exist.

So what about the very human-like Neanderthals and Denisovans found in the fossil record? Are they one of the many missing links? The answer is no. Neanderthals and Denisovans are physically the same as modern humans. They are as genetically and physically different from chimps and apes as modern humans are today. Science is assured of this and this is not in dispute.

So who or what were they? The scientific jury is still out regarding any absolutes regarding who or what these species were and their relationship to modern humans. The first school of thought is that they are descendants of Adam and Eve and therefore no different than modern humans today. Therefore the supposed few percent of our DNA inherited, or shared, from them makes sense and is expected according to this school of thought.

One of the main potential problems with this view is the dating of fossil remains. The dating of Neanderthal and Denisovan fossil remains are in the 40,000 BC to 250,000 BC range, which is well beyond the approximate 4000 BC biblical dating for Adam and Eve. However, this brings into play the accuracy of carbon dating used to date the fossils. The stable form of carbon, carbon-12, is abundant in green plants. An unstable form of carbon, carbon-14, is a naturally occurring radioactive isotope formed in the atmosphere and also makes its way into green plants. Therefore, when a living being, such as humans or animals, eat green plants, they ingest both carbon-12 and carbon-14 contained in the plants. When the plant or species die, the carbon-14 slowly decays into carbon-12. By measuring the relative carbon-14 and carbon-12 levels in the fossil remains and knowing the half-life of carbon-14, and the relative initial ratio between the two forms of carbon in the plants, an estimate of how long the living being has been dead can be estimated.

Although carbon dating is based on solid underlying physics, it uses erroneous assumptions. The first erroneous assumption concerns the amount of carbon in our living biosphere. The flood during Noah's time would have destroyed and buried huge amounts of living plants, and therefore carbon-12. Consequently prior to the flood, the concentration of carbon-12 to carbon-14 would have been correspondingly much higher than today. Since carbon dating is based on the relative amounts of carbon-12 to carbon-14 in a test specimen, this would result in errors in dating. Another erroneous assumption is that the atmospheric concentration of radioactive carbon-14 is constant. The earth's magnetic field, which shields us from cosmic rays that create carbon-14 in our atmosphere, is progressively getting weaker. Therefore, the atmospheric level of carbon-14 is progressively getting higher. Hence, the older a fossil actually is, the much lower its original level of carbon-14 would have been at death compared to our current atmosphere, and the much older apparent date would be assigned to it by carbon dating. The older the specimen, the larger the error. Another erroneous assumption is a constant rate of carbon-14 decay, which has been shown to be not true. Still further, problems with carbon dating include contamination of the sample during handling and leaching of carbon into the sample in the ground. Consequently, carbon dating is suspect for absolute dating of objects, and the older the object is, the larger the potential error.

The second school of thought concerning Neanderthal and Denisovan is they are distinct, separate species from modern humans, without souls, that predated the creation of Adam and Eve. These beings existed on the earth for a while and then became extinct, just like dinosaurs. Supporting this theory are studies indicating no genetic connection between modern humans and Neanderthals. One such study is from Carlos Bustamante and his colleagues at Stanford University in 2016 who concluded, "We've never observed the Neanderthal Y chromosome DNA in any human sample ever tested."[8] Not a few percent as previously reported by others, but absolutely zero.

If this school of thought is correct concerning Neanderthal and Denisovan being separate species from modern humans, why did they become extinct? Could it be they fell victim to the negative effects of gene mutation? We have measured human genome's mutation rate over the six thousand years of humankind's existence. We are reaching the point where gene mutation is causing significant problems, such as cancer, and if uncontrolled, it will eventually lead to our extinction. Could it be Neanderthal and Denisovan, who supposedly existed for two hundred thousand years, simply became extinct from genetic mutations? If we are seeing problems with gene mutation after six thousand years, imagine the health problems after two hundred thousand years.

So, just who are these ancient beings, and are they a separate species who died off before modern humans, or are they in our human lineage and are descendants of Adam and Eve? There is not a consensus in either the scientific or theological fields. Further genome and scientific studies in the near future may lead to further insight to just who these ancient beings were and how we are related to them. What is certain, though, is anatomically speaking Neanderthal, Denisovan, and modern humans did not descend from chimps and apes as there are a multitude of missing links in the fossil chain connecting the groups.

Let's now turn our attention fully to DNA and the human genome studies providing amazing support for the biblical dating of humankind to six thousand years ago. The human genome is the complete set of nuclear DNA instructions in each person. There are 3.2 billion base pairs or instructions in the human genome. These DNA instructions are contained within two sets of twenty-three chromosomes within every cell of the human body (except for hair and fingernails). One twenty-three-chromosome set is inherited from the mother, and one twenty-three-chromosome set from the father. The female DNA is often referred to as X chromosome and the male DNA as Y due to the shape the tightly twisted DNA forms inside the cell.

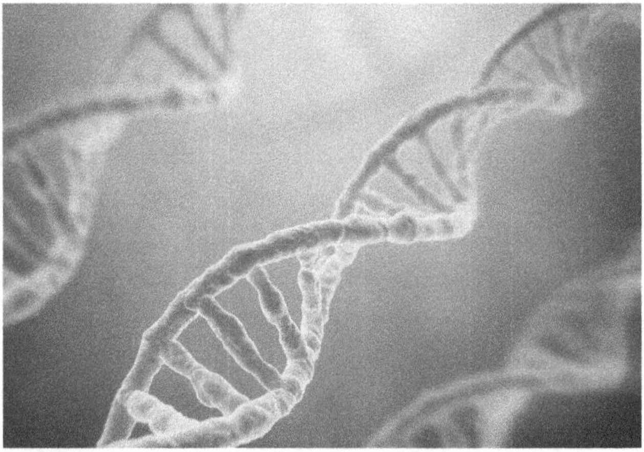

Figure 4.1: DNA strands

Until recent times, the medical and scientific tools and knowhow to map out the complete DNA of an organism, or genome, did not exist. But great strides have been made in recent times in this regard. In 1995, bacteria, with its 1.8 million base pairs, was the first organism to have its complete genome sequenced. The first animal, a worm, was sequenced in 1998, followed by the lab mouse in 2002.[9]

The most heralded genome study to date is the multibillion-dollar international Human Genome Project, or HGP, that started in 1990 and finished with the sequencing of the entire 3.2 billion base pairs of the human genome for the first time ever in 2003.[10] Other human genome studies spawned out of the original HGP, such as the ENCODE Project and the International HapMap Project. In addition, the complete genome mapping of monkeys, orangutans, gorillas, and chimpanzees has been completed. Although the intent of the original studies was for medical purposes, these studies have given many unintended, and intended, answers regarding the origin of humankind and unexpected support of the biblical account regarding the origin and timing of humankind.

So, what are some of these answers? First, as expected, humans do share a significant amount of DNA sequencing with apes and chimps. This is completely expected because if you anatomically look at an ape or chimp, we share a lot of similar-looking body parts. Therefore, you would expect to see a lot of similar DNA sequencing. Historically, it has been widely publicized that humans and chimps share 98 percent of their DNA. More recently, by the same metrics, this number appears to be more in line with 96 percent or twice the number of DNA differences.[11] However, these values do not encompass the entire genome, only a select portion. In 2010, and in subsequent studies, it has been shown that the Y chromosome DNA similarity of humans and chimps was actually less than 70 percent.[12] This equates to millions and millions of genetic letter differences between the humans and chimp. This is significant because there simply is not enough time between when evolutionists say humans and chimps genetically departed from each other and the mutation rate for each species to account for these millions of mutations. This one fact by itself refutes evolution of humans from apes.

Further, common genetic sequencing does not imply common descent; it implies a common designer. As an engineer, one of my existential pleasures is designing new products. Being able to create something new to fill a need or niche with just the right combination of elements to meet a specific need or usage is satisfying. If you were to look at my created products, you would clearly see common design. The design elements and features that work well in one application sometimes work equally well in other applications. Hence, you could look at some of my product designs and see this evidence of "common designer." So too in the living world. Common DNA sequencing is just one telltale sign that points to a common designer for life using common design features across multiple species.

A current hotbed of research activity concerns the DNA mutation rate in humans used to back calculate the age of the human race. To understand these results, though, a basic understanding regarding cell and DNA replication during reproduction is needed. A vital feature of DNA is its ability to replicate itself. This process resembles a zipper being unzipped and then each half of the zipper being zipped back up with a new paired partner. The DNA splits in half, and each half side of the DNA strand matches up with a mating duplicate strand of its original partner, and the two new strands are zipped back together, thus forming two identical strands of the original DNA from the original one. This is necessary for cell duplication, so the living organism can not only grow but also reproduce. In this process of duplication of the DNA strand, however, rare mutations can and do occur whereby the resulting DNA strand is not an exact copy of the original. Although rare, this occurs even though each half of the split DNA strand defines exactly what the other mating half must be.

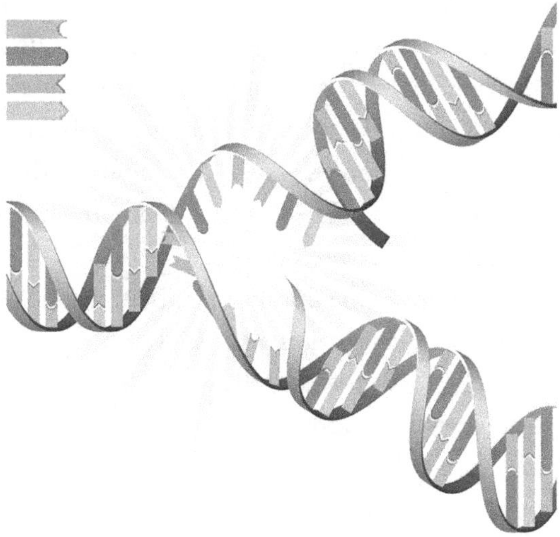

Figure 4.2: DNA replication

In addition to the forty-six chromosomes discussed above, there is another small part of DNA only inherited from our mothers. This DNA is held in unique circular strands in small, tubular packets called mitochondria and is located outside of the nucleus of the cell. Mitochondrial DNA or mtDNA is only passed from mothers to their children and is not passed from the father to the children. The mutation rate for mtDNA is lower than other DNA, but it can be accurately measured. For this reason, mtDNA mutation rates are mainly what are studied to back calculate the age of the human race.

Although a really low value, there is a constant increase in the number of DNA mutations that occurs during reproduction for each generation. So your grandparents would have had a certain number of mutations in their DNA. When they produced your parents, the number of mutations would have been increased by a certain amount. In turn, when your parents produced you, the number of mutations in your DNA would have been increased again by this same amount, and so on and so forth.

The so-called "molecular clock" or "genetic clock" is based on this constant increase in number of mutations occurring during DNA reproduction for each generation. By knowing the mutation rate per generation, and the mutation differences between modern humans and their mutation-free ancestors, along with an estimate of the average time span between generations, the age of modern humans as a species can be back calculated.

For example, suppose the number of mutations in certain DNA is found to be one per generation and modern humans exhibit two hundred mutations. This would tell us modern humans are two hundred generations removed from their mutation-free ancestor. Further, if we assume the average age between generations is thirty years, then we would multiply two hundred mutations per generation times thirty years per generation and come up with an overall age estimate of six thousand years.

The problem with this technique is that it can be, and is, misused. Until recently, factual empirical data concerning the mutation rate was not available. Therefore, it was back calculated based on assumed dates of fossils fitting evolutionary thinking. Hence it was a sort of dirty little secret involving circular logic to the uninformed or casual reader and seemed to reaffirm humans evolved from a common ancestor with apes millions of years ago. With the completion of the Human Genome Project, however, tools and techniques are now available to enable detailed DNA studies to empirically determine the mutation rate.

With the state-of-the-art tools, what have qualified researchers found? One of the first conclusions reached is the genetic differences between any two individuals alive today is much smaller than originally thought. This directly implies the age of the human race is much younger than originally thought. Modern humans are not millions or even hundreds of thousands of years old, as claimed by evolutionists. Modern humans are less than ten thousand years old.

One such early secular study, published in 1997 by Thomas J. Parsons et al. (eleven researchers), titled "A high observed substitution rate in the human mitochondrial DNA control region" states, "The observed substitution rate reported here is very high compared to rates inferred from evolutionary studies."[13] In other words, this early DNA study by evolutionary-minded researchers countered their groupthink regarding what the observed mutation (substitution) rate should be based on evolutionary thinking. Further, they state, "Using our empirical rates to calibrate the mtDNA molecular clock would result in an age of the mtDNA MRCA (most recent common ancestor—aka Eve) of only ~6,500 years ago." This secular, evolutionary supporting research study dating of the origin of humankind to sixty-five hundred years ago agrees quite nicely with the biblical dating for Adam and Eve of six thousand years ago.

A more recent research by Dr. Nathaniel T. Jeanson, combined the raw test results of three other recent mutation studies (Guo et al. 2013, Rebolledo-Jaramillo et al. 2014, and Ding et al. 2015) to achieve a larger sample size and then applied statistical analysis to the results.[14] Based on whole mitochondrial DNA genome mutation rates, he computed the 95 percent confidence bands for the DNA differences expected after six thousand years and arrived at 20-79 base pair differences. The actual DNA data came in at 38-40 base pair differences, almost squarely in the middle of the predicted range, thus indicating humankind is only six thousand years old.

Another research group, Jacob A. Tennessen et al. (twenty-three researchers), published their findings in 2012 titled, *"Evolution and Functional Impact of Rare Coding Variation from Deep Sequencing of Human Exomes."*[15] In their paper, they describe the discovery of a recent acceleration of the human population growth starting 5,115 years ago. This aligns with the biblical account and dating for Noah and the flood.

Still other researchers (Dr. John C. Sanford and Dr. Robert Carter) statistically analyzed over eight hundred human mitochondrial sequences from around the world to reconstruct a representation of Eve's original DNA sequence.[16] They determined the average human is only twenty-two mutations removed from the original Eve mitochondrial sequence while some individuals were as much as one hundred. Based on a recent study indicating a 0.5 per generation mutation rate for the mitochondrial sequence, they concluded, "It would only require 200 generations (less than 6,000 years) to accumulate one hundred mutations." Again, this aligns with biblical dating for the origin of humankind.

So what does all of this mean? First, the factual, scientific DNA evidence clearly indicates humans and chimps did not descend from a common ancestor. We are not here as the result of Darwinian evolution. We are a totally different species from orangutans, gorillas, and chimps. Sure, humans share a lot of DNA with chimps, but that points to a common designer who used similar building blocks for our physical design. Further consider the same metrics showing we share 96 percent of our genes with chimps would also show we share about 90 percent of our genes with cats, 85 percent with mice, 80 percent with cows, 61 percent with fruit flies, 60 percent with chickens, and 60 percent with bananas![17] Second, per worldwide mtDNA studies, modern humans are only about six thousand years old as a species, just as the Bible indicates. Coincidence?

Chapter 5

Are We Spiritually Evolved Apes?

4000 BC: Bible Day 6

As an engineer, I have gained a reputation over the years as a problem solver. Consequently, from time to time I get thrown some rather curious technical problems to solve. Such was the case with a start of production of a new product in Australia. This particular product had passed through all normal product and manufacturing development and associated validation testing. The company was ramping up for production when an intermittent problem appeared with a confirmation test at the production facility. The confirmation test, which was not an industry standard test of any type, consisted of filling a container with an extremely cold liquid and then dropping it on a cement slab from a fixed height. If the container remained intact, it passed, and if it leaked, it was deemed bad even though the test itself had no direct correlation to actual usage.

Although I had no previous knowledge or involvement with such a product, I found myself on a plane headed to Australia to solve this problem. When I arrived, rather than heading to the hotel to recoup from the long flight, I headed straight to the plant. Once there, it came to light this company had flown in people from all over the world and from all different technical disciplines to determine the cause of this problem and correct it as soon as possible. The plant was crawling with so-called experts who were scouring the incoming material and manufacturing processes in an attempt to figure out the source of the problem. It also came to light they had been at it for weeks.

Rather than focus on the materials and processes, I started with the measurement system itself, the test. If it is not right, then everything else based on it is moot. On my arrival, I simply observed the test operator and the test procedure as the tests were conducted. Test after test ticked by as the operator would prepare and then test a sampling of the containers from the manufacturing plant. Not a single failure.

Then it came time for second shift, and although dog tired at this point from having been up well over twenty-four hours, I stayed and observed the second shift operator. He had a very outgoing personality, and we struck up a lively conservation right away. Soon he was offering to bring in a grill the next evening to put a "roo on the barbie" so I could experience what kangaroo really tasted like.

In the midst of our conversations, I kept close tabs on his procedures while he was conducting the test. What became readily apparent to me was that he was not following the established test procedures. The procedures called for filling the container with the cold fluid and then putting the filled container inside a holding chamber until it stabilized to the controlled temperature of the chamber prior to testing. The cold fluid put into the container was much colder than the test specified, and we all know what happens to materials when they become extremely cold; they become extremely brittle. Well this operator was also a smoker. Rather than wait the allotted time before pulling the container from the holding chamber, he would rush the procedure and test too soon when the fluid and container were much too cold and had not stabilized to the warmer holding chamber temperature so he could have a smoke between tests. Viola! Problem found. There was absolutely nothing wrong with the materials or manufacturing process used to make the containers; they simply were not being tested per procedures. The so-called experts simply failed to look at the obvious. With their bias and expertise in their various technical fields, they had missed it and also failed to realize all the failures came from second shift, which in itself was a huge clue.

Differentiating between humans and apes, or humans and mere animals, is a lot like this. We tend to overlook the obvious, even though it can be right in front of us. What makes humans unique from animals? From a physical sense, we share common design features and parts with other animals, such as head, eyes, ears, arms, hands, legs, and feet. This is evidence of a common designer. We can see these features in a macroscopic sense physically with our eyes or see it in a microscopic sense in our DNA. But is there an aspect to humans that sets us apart from other created living beings on earth? The Bible says a definite yes. We humans are more than the sum of the physical molecules and cells that make up our bodies. We have a nonphysical spirit or soul, or in the original Hebrew language of the Old Testament of the Bible, a *neshama*.

6000 Years Ago: Day 6

> The Lord God formed the man from the dust of the ground and breathed into his nostrils the breath of life, and the man became a living being. (Genesis 2:7)
>
> If there is a natural body, there is also a spiritual body. So it is written: "The first man Adam became a living being"; the last Adam, a life-giving spirit. (1 Corinthians 15:45)

In the original Hebrew language of the Old Testament, there are two words for soul and spirit, nephesh and neshama. The first, nephesh, means living being with a free choice. The first living things of God's creation, plants, do not have a nephesh. The next level of living things, animals, have a nephesh. Animals have the ability to make choices, although it is generally governed by instinct or environmental conditioning. The third level of living things, humankind, was given a spiritual soul or neshama. Neshama is the nonphysical soul or spirit the Bible talks about humans possessing throughout the Bible. Only human beings have a neshama. Per the Bible, our neshama does not cease to exist at our physical death but is eternal.

In Genesis 2:7, the word *breath* was translated from the original Hebrew scripture from the word *neshama*. The last word in the sentence, "living being," was translated from "nephesh." So in the context of the original Hebrew language, Genesis 2:7 could be paraphrased as:

> God breathed into Adam's nostrils his spirit and he became a living being with free will.

Per the Bible, you and I have a spirit or soul, a neshama that separates us from all other created beings on earth. Our soul will live for eternity.

With that in mind, let's examine the evidence to see if there is something more to us than just our physical being. Is there an aspect to the human mind, soul, or spirit that cannot be explained by naturalistic mechanisms and would point toward a divine creator, giving further credibility to the Bible and the Christian faith? In other words, does: human life = physical body + nonphysical soul?

We will start with the simplest and then progress to the more abstract. The first area to consider is human thought itself. The father of modern philosophy, Rene Descartes declared, "Cogito ergo sum" or translated, "I think, therefore I am."[1] The fact that we think, and can consider our own existence, is evidence in itself there is a separation between the brain and mind as Descartes believed. As even Darwinist philosopher Michael Ruse confessed, "Why should a bunch of atoms have thinking ability?... No one, certainly not the Darwinian as such, seems to have any answer to this... The point is that there is no scientific answer."[2]

How could Darwinian evolution possibly explain the creation of thought? There is not an evolutionary stepping stone process that could explain how innate atoms and molecules could evolve into conscious thought. Even with a starting point of the first living cell, bacteria, how does that progress into human thought? It is inconceivable. Thought all by itself points away from evolution and toward an intelligent creator, God.

Next, reflect for a moment on the fact that human beings seek God. Universally and throughout the ages, all human races, tribes, and nations have sought out God. Whether it is Europeans settling into the Americas, or African pygmies on the desert plain, or tribesmen in Papua New Guinea, they have all sought out after a creator God. Other created animals, such as monkeys and apes, do not exhibit this characteristic. Or at least we have never detected any form of worship in a nonhuman animal. Where does this desire or instinct come from? It is as if it is preprogrammed into our DNA that we are to consider, reflect upon, and seek God. Why? One logical answer is there is a creator God who indeed preprogrammed us to seek him.

Yet another intriguing area of human thought pointing to a creator God and separating us from other animals is morality. Think about times when you have overheard children having arguments. You will hear things like:

> "How would you like it if I did that to you?"
> "That's my seat. I was there first."
> "Leave him alone. He isn't hurting you."
> "Give me some of your treats. I gave you some of mine."
> "Come on, you promised."

Take time to pause and reflect on the depth of what is being implied here with these statements. Without being stated explicitly, these statements are appealing to a standard of behavior one person expects the other person to abide by. Without formal training, these universal rules of behavior are recognized and adhered to almost magically. The other person does not say, "Your reasoning does not make sense," or "Forget your rules." Almost always the other child tries to make sure they do not go against this standard, or if they do, try to justify their behavior with a special excuse. Why is that?

Like seeking God, universally and throughout the ages, all human races, tribes, and nations have a sense of morality and ethics. Notice I did not say all humans act or behave morally. We certainly do not. But even in the most hardened hearts, there is generally a sense of what is morally right and wrong. Where does this sense come from? It is not natural in a physical world.

One is left to conclude that humans' sense of morality, like seeking God, seems preprogrammed into our DNA by a moral God. If in fact we were made in God's image, then this would explain this innate sense of right and wrong.

Yet another area concerning human thought giving credibility to a creator is the issue of brain versus self. Is there a difference between the physical brain and a nonphysical self, accounting for our conscious? Darwin and physicalists (those claiming the only existing substance is physical) claim there is no separation between the brain and self. To them, the brain is solely responsible for consciousness. In other words, everything is physical. But if physicalism is true, then consciousness could not exist.

Consider the following logic from J.P. Moreland.[3]

First, if physicalism is true and everything is physical, then everything can be described entirely from a third-person point of view. But since we clearly have first-person subjective points of view, physicalism cannot be true. For instance, an individual person could not have individual experiences and emotions. The reason would be everything is physical and all observations would be exactly the same whether viewed from that individual person's viewpoint or any other persons. But since we know they obviously are not the same, then physicalism cannot be true.

Second, if physicalism is true, there could be no such thing as free will because matter would be completely governed by the laws of nature. Suppose you are in a room and decide to get up and turn the lights on or off, or both. If physicalism was true, then your action would be totally governed by the laws of physics. But your impetus to turn the lights on or off may have been driven totally on a whim and certainly not in obedience of the law of gravity or the first law of thermodynamics. You consciously decided to turn the lights on or off and this governed your action, not the laws of physics as mandated by physicalism.

Third, if physicalism is true, there would be no near-death experiences since everything is physical and there could not be no disembodied intermediate state. Yet we know there are thousands of near-death experiences that occur each day throughout the world.

To further investigate this issue of the physical and nonphysical self, let's turn to medical studies for answers and consider the work of Dr. Wilder Penfield (1891–1976), who is considered the father of modern neurosurgery. Penfield pioneered mapping the human brain and functions using electrical simulations.[4] In fact, his maps are used to this day. Originally Penfield was not a believer in dualism, or this idea of a physical and nonphysical brain, when he started his work in neurology. He thought consciousness was a result of neural activities in the brain and there was no difference between the brain and self.

To study physical versus nonphysical brain activity, Penfield electrically stimulated the motor cortex of conscious patients and instructed them to keep one hand from moving. When electrically stimulating one hand to move, the other hand of the patient would grab the moving hand and try to keep it still. Therefore one hand was under control of the electric stimulation and the other hand under control of the patient's mind. Penfield reasoned in addition to a physical brain activity, there is also a nonphysical aspect with the patient's brain causing action. Through his own work, Penfield changed his opinion concerning the two and believed they were in fact separate entities. Per Penfield, "There is no place... where electrical stimulation will cause a patient to believe or to decide. That's because those functions originate in the conscious self, not the brain."

Near-death experiences (NDEs) are yet another source of scientific medical study. There are 774 near death experiences in the United States alone each day.[5] There are many books and movies based on true life NDEs, such as, *Heaven is for Real, 90 Minutes in Heaven, The Boy Who Came Back from Heaven*, and *Proof of Heaven: A Neurosurgeon's Journey into the Afterlife.*

NDEs have been studied around the globe, such as at the University of Southampton in England based on patients who survived cardiac arrest. Or at the University of Connecticut where Dr. Kenneth Ring, PhD, professor emeritus of psychology, studied cases of blind people who reported visually accurate accounts during NDE. And at the University of Washington, where Dr. Melvin Morse, associate professor of pediatrics, studies NDE of children.[6, 7, 8] Collectively these NDE studies have provided evidence consciousness continues after a person's brain has stopped functioning and has been declared clinically dead.

In 2001, British physician Sam Parnia and neuropsychiatrist Peter Fenwick published their study in the journal *Resuscitation.* Their study, as mentioned above, was based on sixty-three heart attack victims who were declared dead and later revived and interviewed. Parnia, once a skeptic, speculated the brain might serve as a mechanism to manifest the mind, like a TV manifesting pictures and sounds from electromagnetic waves in the air.[9] His study provided evidence that consciousness continues after a person's brain has stopped functioning and has been declared clinically dead.

Perhaps the NDE that literally is as close to a scientifically controlled experiment as one could imagine occurred to Pam Reynolds.[10] Pam was a singer and songwriter, and her company

Southern Tracks has recorded music from such groups and artists as Bruce Springsteen, Pearl Jam, and REM. In 1991 it was discovered Pam had a large, life-threatening aneurysm on her brain. She underwent highly risky surgery to correct this problem whereby her body was chilled, the blood drained from her head, her skull was cut open, the aneurysm removed, and then she was brought back to life. During this surgery Pam's eyes were taped shut and molded speakers were placed in her ears, playing loud clicking sounds so the doctors could monitor her brain stem activity.

Pam was completely unconscious during the surgery. She had no brain activity, as indicated by her flat-lined EEG monitor. She had no response to the clicks in her ears, and she had no blood flow to the brain. Pam was physically dead from the neck up! Amazingly while in this state during surgery she experienced the following:

> She heard a noise that "sounded like a natural D" and then "popped out of the top of her head."
> She looked down on the operating table and could see 20 people.
> She could see the Midas Rex bone saw in the surgeon's hand and could describe intricate details.
> She heard the doctors talking and could recall details of their conversation.
> She chatted with her dead grandmother and uncle, who later escorted her back to the operating room.
> She heard the Eagles song "Hotel California" playing in the surgery room as she re-entered her body.

She recalled all of this following the surgery despite being clinically brain dead during these events. With the exception of visiting with her dead relatives, all other physical events, equipment, and music she described were accurate descriptions of what took place in the surgery room. Because of the extraordinary nature of the experience, she was examined by multiple professionals, who interrogated her and concluded her testimony and experience was real.

With such a controlled procedure and her experience and observations defying normal explanation, one is left to conclude she really did see and experience those things apart from her body. The only explanation is Pam's brain and self were two separate entities. The brain was dead during the procedure, but her conscious self was not, and she was able to experience much of the procedure from an external perspective apart from her body. Pam's medical procedure and experience provides authenticated evidence of a separate physical and nonphysical self, just as the Bible claims.

Is there still further evidence of the human soul separating humans from all other animals? Yes, evidence of humans' souls expresses its spirituality through culture. Although the soul is nonphysical by definition, the spirituality it brings about is clearly evident in human culture. Evolutionists claim that humankind is millions of years old. If so, why does the richness of human culture spring to life only six thousand years ago in line with the creation of the first beings with a soul, Adam and Eve, as the Bible states? Coincidence again? If humankind is millions or even hundreds of thousands of years old, we should see evidence of rich culture with these supposedly ancient human beings. But we do not, we see human culture springing to life just six thousand years ago. Any guesses about when writing came about or when the wheel was invented? Yep, roughly fifty-five hundred years ago.[11, 12] Interestingly, they both first appeared in the Mesopotamia region, where the Bible indicates the garden of Eden was located, as well as the early Bible patriarchs.

Consider the vast difference between human beings of the six thousand years old or less vintage, with those the evolutionists point to as stepping stones to humans. Prior to six thousand years ago, all created beings struggled to just survive. There was no richness of culture indicative of human spirituality. Contrast this against the most recent six thousand years, which marks the appearance of soulful humankind per the Bible. Since six thousand years ago, humans have created cell phones and computers, built telescopes to gaze into the far reaches of the universe to see the first light from the beginning of time, built scanning electron microscopes to peer into the human DNA, created planes flying faster than the speed of sound, built spaceships to travel to other planets, created medicines and medical procedures such as heart transplants, pacemakers, and artificial limbs, built skyscrapers reaching into the clouds, built cities with infrastructures to support millions of people, built massive dams to harness water and convert the energy into electricity, have libraries containing thousands of books with written language, document history through written word, create and play symphony music, create an endless variety of gourmet foods, create an endless variety of clothing, come together worldwide every four years for the Olympics, think and interact about abstract thoughts, love unconditionally, and worship God. Of course, this is just the tip of the iceberg for what humankind has done in the last six thousand years. There is no comparison between the last six thousand years and the previous millions of years. The Bible states God created humans with souls in his image and the results are very evident. Humans are eternally different than animals. Let's not overlook the obvious.

The Bible states humankind has a soul distinct from the physical body, which separates us from all other living beings. This can be observed and is supported by scientific studies, in a variety of areas. Coincidence?

Chapter 6

What Yom Is It?

13.8 Billion Years to 4000 BC: Bible Days 1-6

Sometimes timing can be everything. I was reminded of this during my graduate studies in Finland. As part of my master thesis, I traveled to Finland to study cogeneration and district heating at power plants across their country. Cogeneration is a system whereby waste heat energy from the generation of electricity at power plants is used to heat homes and buildings.

My flight to Finland landed in Helsinki late in the evening in early January. A graduate student from Lappeenranta University picked me up at the airport and drove me during the middle of the night across the snow-blanketed countryside to the outskirts of the city of Lappeenranta. There I was given a small cabin to lodge in for the first period of my stay. It was a short walk from the university and on the banks of a large frozen lake. I was warned not to walk across the frozen lake as the other side was the Soviet Union and two people had been grabbed by them the previous week.

So after a very long day, off to sleep I fell in this Norman Rockwell–looking winter wonderland cabin with deep snow covering everything outside. When I woke up, it was early afternoon the next day. With it being the weekend and the university closed, I was eager to visit the city and get my sightseeing out of the way, so when Monday rolled around, I would be ready to immerse myself solely into my studies. After a hot shower and change of clothes, I was ready to hit the town. Besides, I was very hungry at this point as well. The city had a public transportation busing system traveling to the university, and after figuring out which bus and what time it arrived, I headed to the bus stop, camera in tow. After a half-hour ride on the bus, and the various stops along the way, I made it to the city. When I stepped off the bus, however, the sun was beginning to set and daylight for picture taking was fading fast. You see, Finland is in the far northern climate, and with the tilt of the earth's axis from the sun, it has only a few hours of daylight in the winter. My picture-taking trip would have to wait for another day. My intent and plan were good, but my timing was terrible. As I said, sometimes timing can be everything.

Before proceeding on in our timeline, we are going to pause for a chapter and examine another timing-related issue: dating. No, not the male-female love kind but the twenty-four hours, 365 days in the year kind. We will first examine the beginning of time up to the creation of humankind. Then we will look forward from the creation of humankind to the present time. In the process we want to explore what the Bible says about dates relative to our current understanding to see from yet another perspective the credibility of the Bible.

Let's turn our attention back to the Bible and the beginning of time as described in the first book of the Bible, Genesis. Central to this study is the interpretation of just one word appearing throughout this chapter. The word in the English language is *day*. The word appearing in the original Hebrew language in the text is *yom*. Yom is like day in that it does not necessarily mean a twenty-four-hour period, such as in "back in the day."

Consider that the ancient Hebrew language has only eighty-seven hundred words and the English language has five hundred thousand words.[1] Therefore, out of necessity, words in the Hebrew language have more multiple meanings than in the English language.

Yom is no exception. The meaning of the word *yom* in the Hebrew language can mean:[2]

1. A period of daylight time
2. Twelve-hour daylight period
3. Twenty-four-hour period
4. Lengthy, but finite period

Perhaps the biggest concern for interpreting yom in the first chapter of Genesis as the last definition, "lengthy, but finite period," concerns death and all the theological implications of death once it enters the world. From a biblical perspective, if yom is interpreted as a "lengthy, but finite period," then this implies death for plants and animals entered the world prior to Adam sinning. Death for humankind, however, and all the theological ramifications it brings about per the Bible, enters the world at the time of Adam's sin.

Consider, though, that plant death would have occurred prior to the fall of humankind due to sin in any interpretation, whether yom is interpreted as twenty-four hours or billions of years, as animals would have fed on plants during day 6, inevitably killing some of the plants. There would have also been death with fish as well as most fish eat other fish for food. Also consider Adam gave carnivore names to some of the animals he named, indicating they killed other animals to feed.[3] Finally, God warned Adam death would come to him if he ate from the tree of knowledge of good and evil. How would Adam know and appreciate what God meant if he did not see or experience death firsthand before God's warning?

Now consider Adam and his first day of life schedule. If yom six is interpreted as a twenty-four-hour earth-based time period, he had a very full first day: he was created by God, he was put in the garden of Eden, he observed and named all of the animals, he realized all the animals had a helper or mate except for him, he was put in a deep sleep, and Eve was created from his rib. If yom is interpreted as a lengthy but finite period, then the timing of the events in the life of Adam seem more plausible—duly noting, however, all things are possible with God.

Next consider the pattern of how the word yom is used in the first chapter of Genesis in the Bible: "And there was evening and morning—the first/second/third/fourth/fifth/sixth yom." Since a twenty-four-hour day period is based on one rotation of the earth on its axis, and the earth did not exist for the first two yoms since it was formless swirling gases, interpretation of the word *yom* as two earth rotations, or forty-eight earth hours, for the first two periods of time seems very odd.

Finally, let's consider dinosaurs again. If yom was a twenty-four-hour period, dinosaurs would have been created on the sixth day. Under this scenario, dinosaurs and humans coexisted. This also implies dinosaurs would have been on Noah's ark and therefore lived among humans after the flood for many years before they became extinct. This seems nonsensical. There is no substantiated evidence humans and dinosaurs coexisted on the earth at the same time. Likewise, there are also no obvious mentions of dinosaurs in the Bible even though people have looked to such scripture as Job 40:15 where the use of the term *behemoth* is used. It likely refers to animals such as elephants. Granted the Bible is written for the main purpose of instructions for our eternal salvation and consequently there are many types of animals not mentioned in the Bible. But it is curious that such large animals as dinosaurs, if they coexisted with humans, would not have been clearly mentioned. It is also noteworthy dinosaurs are also not mentioned in any ancient secular writings.

The scientific understanding concerning dinosaurs is they appeared around 225 million years ago and became extinct around 66 million years ago. They lived on earth when the surface of the earth was much different than today, with extensive swampy areas. This allowed some species to reach massive size despite earth's gravity by living and wading in water to take weight off their skeletal structure. Dinosaurs became extinct long before humans appeared on earth. Humankind first found out about dinosaurs only two hundred years ago with the discovery of fossil remains. This means during the period the Bible was written, the Bible authors would have had no firsthand knowledge of dinosaurs. If yom is interpreted as a lengthy but finite period, this makes sense. Dinosaurs could have come and gone with humankind created afterward, and humankind did not even know about dinosaurs until two hundred years ago, all within the sixth yom. This also explains the lack of mention of dinosaurs in secular writing from the dawn of humankind until two hundred years ago since humankind simply did not know dinosaurs ever existed.

One final note regarding yom concerns the seventh yom. Consistent with the first six periods of time, yoms one through six, the Bible does not state in Genesis, "And there was evening and morning—the seventh yom." There is no mention of the seventh yom. This seems to suggest we are currently living in the seventh yom or period. It is also worth noting that from a biblical perspective, the number seven signifies completeness. Since we haven't reached the end times as prophesied in the Bible, this would also suggest we are still in the seventh period, or seventh yom.

So what's the correct interpretation of the word *yom* as used in the first chapter of Genesis? Is it a twenty-four-hour earth-based period of time or a lengthy, but finite period of time? Before we answer, let's dig a bit deeper into current scientific dating. The oldest event science has tried to date is the beginning of time itself, which occurred when the universe came into being. This is accomplished by measuring the frequency of the light received from distant stars emitted at the moment of the universe's inception. With a knowledge of how much the frequency of the emitted electromagnetic light wave has been reduced and how fast we are moving apart, it is possible to calculate the time lag. Using this technique, in 2012 NASA's WMAP study estimated the age of the universe to be 13.77 billion years old.[4] Similarly in 2013, the European Planck study estimated the age of the universe to be 13.82 billion years old.[5]

These time scales are well beyond the previously discussed carbon dating. With a carbon-14 half-life of 5,730 years, this technique can only be extended to around 50,000 years.[6] But another technique similar to carbon-14 dating is potassium-argon and rubidium-strontium dating. These isotopes have a much slower decay rate than carbon-14. They are rarely found in objects such as fossils but can occur in the surrounding or adjoining rock layers. By dating the rocks and materials above and below an object, scientists can deduce the approximate age of the layer the object is in and therefore the approximate age of the object.

The age of the earth is determined by aging the rock and material found on it. The oldest known rocks were found in Canyon Diablo located in Arizona, and from radiometric dating have been aged at 4.5 billion years old. Moon rocks, brought back to earth, have also been dated to 4.5 billion years. Other estimates for the age of the earth supporting an age much greater than several thousand years include:

Continental drift rate to form ocean	190 million years old[7]
Erosion of the Grand Canyon	17 million years old[8]
Annual layers in glaciers	750,000 years old[9]
Thickness of coral reefs	176,000 years old[10]
Radiocarbon dating of wood	50,000 years old[11]
Bristlecone pine trees in California	6,000 years old[12]

Figure 6.1: Grand Canyon

In all, the scientific data for the age of the universe and earth from the beginning of time to the appearance of the first humans on the earth appears much greater than six earth-based days. However, is there a possibility God created a world "pre-aged"? Sure, why not? After all, we think of Adam as a fully mature man on his first day of life, not a newborn baby. But the question is, did he?

In case you are wondering concerning the wording "evening and morning" in Genesis somehow expressing or implying a twenty-four-hour day period, the original intent becomes clearer with a bit of examination. The Hebrew word in Genesis interpreted as "evening" and "morning" are *erev* and *boker*. Their original meaning was not evening and morning but rather chaos and order respectively. God increasingly reduced entropy, or in common terms, disorder, during the creation process whereby he changed chaos into order.

Further, consider in other places in the Bible where the writer was describing twenty-four-hour periods of time such as Moses on Mount Sinai, Noah in the ark, or Jonah in the big fish. The writer used the expression such as "forty days and forty nights" not "forty evenings and forty mornings" to signify a twenty-four-hour period.

Putting this all together, the expressions in the first chapter of Genesis can be interpreted as: "And there was chaos, and there was order—the first/second/third/fourth/fifth/sixth period of time."

Curiosity kills the cat, and curiosity certainly is the nature of an engineer such as myself. So let's dig even deeper. From Einstein's general theory of relativity, it is known the physical location of the clock is vitally important to the observed time. Not all time is the same. Time on earth is different than time on the moon. In fact, the time at each point in space is different due to the time dilation effects of speed and gravity. Suppose the clock during the creation of the universe was not on the earth itself but encompassed all the created universe such as from God's perspective. In this fashion time represents a universal time, and the increments of time are defined per the yom periods in the Genesis account. From this perspective, how would the created time on earth compare to this universal time for yom one through six?

A very interesting correlation can be constructed if we start by accepting the premise that the earth-based age of the universe and the beginning of time is approximately 13.8 billion years old based on the 2012 NASA study and 2013 Planck study. Next, add in the age of the earth as 4.5 billion years old based on radiometric dating and that it solidified to become an actual planet at the start of the third yom. Finally, consider the creation of humankind occurred six thousand years ago at the end of the sixth yom as described in the Bible.

If we take these three points, we can construct a curve fit line through these points to interpolate an approximate timing for each of the six yom periods. So the question is now, what type of relationship to assume between earth based time and universal based time for this curve. If we knew the details of exactly how the universe expanded from a singularity during the big bang with all the masses and expansion speeds involved, we could attempt to mathematically model the impact on relative time. However, many of these details are not known, and the derivation would be quite lengthy and beyond the scope of this book. For our purposes here, a simple third-order polynomial curve fit was used to establish a reasonable curve fit line based on the three data points. The resulting equation is:

$$\text{Time since beginning (billions of years)} = 0.05691 \times \text{yom}^3 - 1.035 \times \text{yom}^2 + 6.457 \times \text{yom}$$

Note: yom in this equation represents the time point at the end of each time period.

So for instance, if we wanted to know how much time elapsed since the beginning of time before the earth was formed, we would calculate it at the end of yom two since the earth was formed at the beginning of yom three. Inserting two into the equation above results in 9.23 billion years. This means the earth was formed 9.23 billion years after the initial big bang. If the universe began 13.77

billion years ago, this means the earth was formed 13.77 minus 9.23, or approximately 4.54 billion years ago.

Using this equation, the following three graphs were generated depicting the correlation between earth-based time and universal based time.

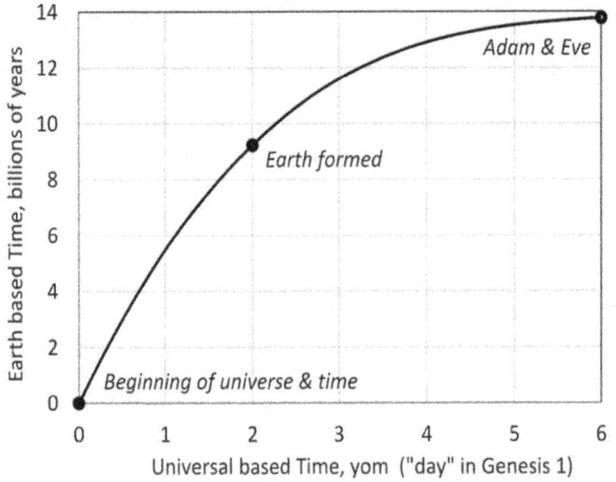

Figure 6.2: Elapsed time since the beginning of the universe

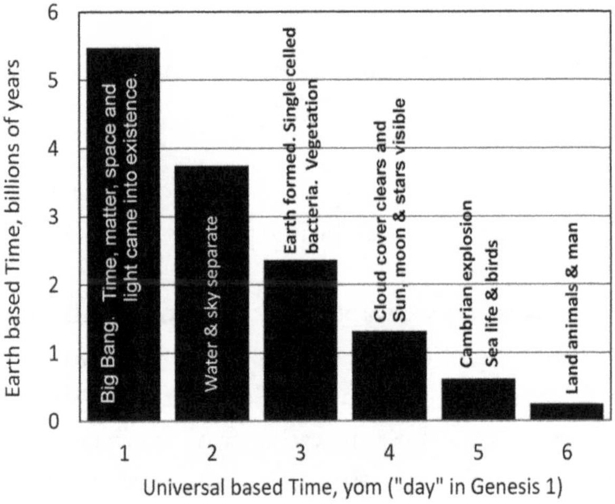

Figure 6.3: Length of each creation period

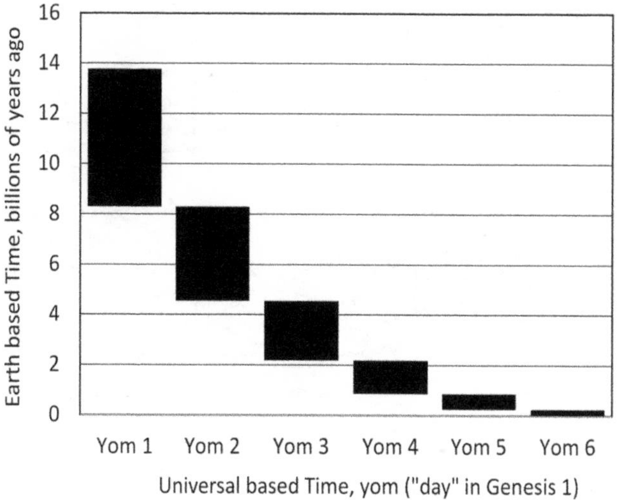

Figure 6.4: Time span of each creation period

So if we interpret the clock location during the first chapter of Genesis to represent a universal time, due to time dilation as predicted by Einstein's General Theory of Relativity, each of the six time periods described in the Bible correlate exactly to six consistent increments of time. Further, the chronological rollout of created matter, plants and life exactly, and correctly, fall into these six time periods. Coincidence?

Bible Day	**Universal Time Increment**	**Earth Time**	**Major Event**
1	1 yom	13.77–8.29 BYA	Creation of matter and light
2	1 yom	8.29–4.54 BYA	Creation of sky
3	1 yom	4.54–2.18 BYA	Creation of earth and plants
4	1 yom	2.18—0.86 BYA	Creation of sun and moon
5	1 yom	0.86–0.25 BYA	Creation of animals
6	1 yom	0.25 BYA—6,000 YA	Creation of man

Figure 6.5: Major creation events during the first six biblical yoms

If we turn back to the subject of dinosaurs, we can see from God's perspective on yom six, dinosaurs were created and became extinct before the creation of humankind even though from an earth-based perspective, these events would have been millions of years apart. In fact, with this timing all the current scientific-based aging studies of events and appearances of species fall neatly in line. Again, coincidence?

This brings us up to the appearance of humankind six thousand years ago per the Bible as we discussed in the last two chapters. Beyond what we discussed, is there even further evidence or proof yom six ended only six thousand years ago and therefore humankind is only six thousand years old? There certainly is: historical human population. By studying population growth and population estimates, we can get yet another indication that humankind is only six thousand years old, as the Bible indicates.

To complete this examination, however, we need to peek chronologically ahead into next chapter's subject of the Old Testament. So, if you don't mind, we will look ahead into the Old Testament a bit and look at yet another facet lending credibility to the dating of humankind of six thousand years, just as the Bible indicates.

The estimated current worldwide human population stands around 7.5 billion, or 7,500,000,000 people.[13] How did we get to this point? According to evolutionists, we arrived at this point after millions of years of human existence. To study this, a mathematical model can be constructed assuming a constant growth rate for the human population up until AD 1600, when the population growth rate exploded to the present. Of course, strictly speaking the growth rate for humans is not constant. Factors such as famines, diseases, and improvements in medicine all serve to alter this rate. However, these numbers do reflect "on average" what it would take to go from two people initially to today's worldwide population.

The graph below is a result of this effort. Because of the compounding nature of population growth, the vertical axis or population axis is shown using a logarithmic scale. With such a scale, constant population growth rates, such as 1 percent per year, plot as a straight line. Two sets of population estimates are shown in the graph. The two sets are for an assumed age of humankind according to evolution theory claiming humankind is one to three million years old.

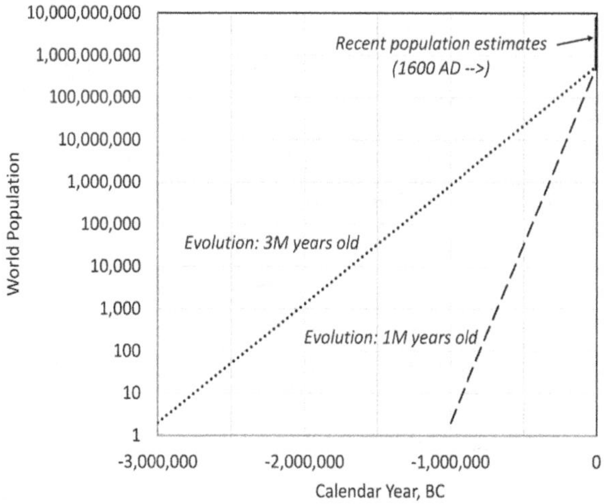

Figure 6.6: Evolution-based population models

The "on average" growth rate for humankind being one to three million years old per evolutionary theory would be between 0.000648 and 0.0019418 percent respectively. This is absurdly low based on population studies of historical human and animal population growths.

With this population model, however, and using population estimates from AD 1600 to the present, we can estimate the total number of people who ever lived. This estimate can be arrived at by integrating the area under the population versus year curve and divide by an assumed average life span, say eighty, to get an estimate of the total worldwide population of those who ever lived. The results of this modeling yields 825 billion people if we assume humankind is one million years old and 5,293 billion people if we assume humankind is three million years old per evolutionary theory. Under this scenario, only 0.14 to 0.91 percent of the total people who ever lived are alive today.

Next, consider the earth has 24.6 million square miles of habitable land mass or 15.8 billion acres.[14] This means if evolution is true and humankind has been around for one to three million years, there have been between 52 and 336 deceased people for every habitable acre of ground on earth! If this is true, the earth should be littered with human remains. But the earth is not. In fact, discovery of human remains is very rare. What does this simple check and information suggest? It suggests that our assumption of humans on the earth for one to three million years must be in gross error.

So what does the Bible say? Portions of the Bible are very detailed regarding genealogy, ages of various patriarchs, and historical events. In fact, you might not be aware of this, but the Bible gives the complete lineage from Adam to Jesus. Try to beat that with your own family tree! From Adam to Jesus there are seventy-six generations. As a quick estimate, if we assume fifty years between each generation during this time period (see information below on early patriarch's age at birth of child) we come up with roughly four thousand years. Since Jesus was born two thousand years ago, this puts the origin of humankind at six thousand years ago.

But the Bible is more detailed than this, and we can refine this estimate. The following table is the listing in chronological order of the patriarch and their child with both the age of the father at the child's birth and his life span as listed in Genesis 5 and 11:

Father	**Life Span** *years*	**Age at Child's Birth** *years*	**Child**
Adam	930	130	Seth
Seth	912	105	Enosh
Enosh	905	90	Kenan
Kenan	910	70	Mahalalel
Machalalel	895	65	Jared
Jared	962	162	Enoch
Enoch	365*	65	Methuselah
Methuselah	969	187	Lamech
Lamech	777	182	Noah
Noah	950	500	Shem
Shem	600	100	Arphaxad
Arphaxad	438	35	Shelah
Shelah	433	30	Eber
Eber	464	34	Peleg
Peleg	239	30	Reu
Reu	239	32	Serug
Serug	230	30	Nahor
Nahor	148	29	Terah
Terah	205	70	Abraham
Abraham	175	100	Isaac
Isaac	180	40	Jacob
Jacob	147	90	Joseph

*The Bible says God took Enoch away and he did not suffer death.

At first blush, the life span of the patriarchs seems outrageous. How could anyone live to be this old? It is also curious that after Noah and the flood the Bible speaks about, the life span of his descendants followed a natural biological decay rate. Quite interesting and to the point of this book, can these claims be underpinned with scientific reasoning or data?

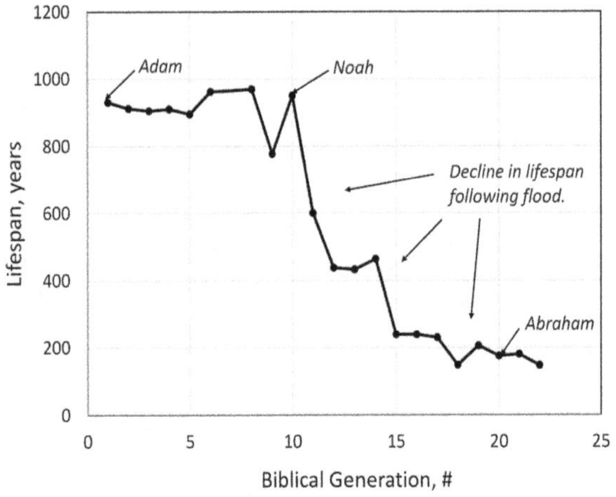

Figure 6.7: Decay in patriarchal life span following flood

Recall there are compounding DNA mutations occurring with every generation. These mutations are harmful to the overall health of the person and lead to a shortened life span. Adam and Eve would have had the perfect, mutation-free DNA. This could explain the initial long life spans starting with Adam. However, there is no discernable decay in the age of the patriarchs from Adam to Noah. It appears fairly constant. But after Noah, there is a very pronounced change as life spans fall off as a biological decay function. One of the known causes of DNA mutations is ultraviolet radiation from the sun. Could there have been a change to the atmosphere and environment before and after the flood contributing to the reduction in life span? Could it be the earth's atmosphere concerning the clouds and water vapor changed after the flood, allowing more ultraviolet radiation to reach the earth after the flood, triggering the mutations and shortened life spans? Further, collaborating evidence to this point is the appearance of the rainbow after the great flood. God gave the rainbow after the flood as a sign of the covenant he would never cut off life with a flood again.

> And God said, "This is the sign of the covenant I am making between me and you and every living creature with you, a covenant for all generations to come. I have set my rainbow in the clouds, and it will be the sign of the covenant between me and the earth. Whenever I bring clouds over the earth and the rainbow appears in the clouds, I will remember my covenant between me and you and all living creatures of every kind. Never again will the waters become a flood to destroy all life. (Genesis 9:13–15)

This implies rainbows did not appear in the skies before the flood. This in turn suggests the atmosphere was much different after the flood. Again, could this change in the atmosphere be linked to increased solar radiation reaching the earth, therefore an increase in DNA mutation, and the resulting reduction in life span clearly seen occurring after the flood?

Whatever the case for this life span decay may be, we can take this type of information from the Bible and construct a population model. First, between Adam and Noah, the patriarchs lived an average of 912 years. Using reference information on growth rates, we can set the earliest rate at 1.0 percent. After Noah there was a significant decay in life spans. We can model this as a decaying function starting out at 1.0 percent and decaying to 0.1 percent by AD 1600 in accordance with the actual growth rate and life span decay listed in the Bible. Further, the growth rate during this period decays proportional to the life span decay from 912 years down to 80 years in AD 1600. From AD 1600 onward, we can use modern population estimates.

From the Bible we have two important dates and events to place on this timeline differing from the evolutionary model. First, Adam and Eve can be placed on this population chart at 4000 BC per biblical dating. Second, the flood that wiped out all of humankind except for the eight people on Noah's ark occurred around 2350 BC. With these dates and the information above, we can construct a first-order population model.

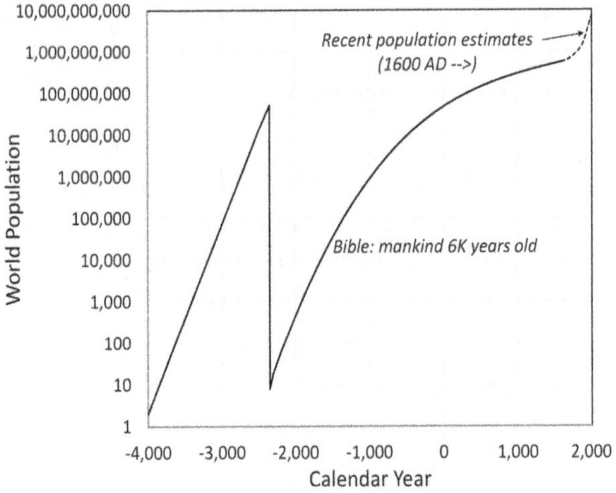

Figure 6.8: Bible-based population model

This population model is based on biblical information. Based on this model, there have only been 14 billion people on earth, of which 7.5 billion, or 54 percent, are alive today. And from a human remains standpoint, this translates into 0.4 remains per acre. Further consider the bulk of the people lived from AD 1600 on under this scenario, and most of their remains are in cemeteries, it should come as no surprise that for someone digging in the ground, or even for a paleontologist intentionally looking for fossils, finding humans remains is extremely rare.

Compiling this information into a single chart, we can compare and contrast the estimates:

Origin of Humankind	Age of Humankind	Total Historical Population	Alive Today	Potential Human Remains
	years	*billion*	*percent*	*remains/acre*
Evolution	3 million	5,293	0.14	336
Evolution	1 million	825	0.91	52
Creation	6 thousand	14	54	0.4

To put these numbers into perspective, consider the US military cemetery, Arlington National Cemetery. It is densely packed, with rows upon rows of four hundred thousand deceased military personnel. Now consider the cemetery is 640 acres.[15] This equates to 641 graves per acre at this site. Therefore, this means if you believe humankind evolved from apes, one to three million years ago, and if you assumed all deceased were buried in a cemetery with a burial density of Arlington National Cemetery, then between 8 to 53 percent of the habitable face of the earth would be covered in cemeteries! Conversely, if you believe in creation, the similar value would be 0.06 percent. So what seems most plausible to you—the evolutionist's one to three million years old age for humankind, or the Bible's six thousand years?

Figure 6.9: Arlington National Cemetery

For centuries, naysayers to the Christian faith have ridiculed the Bible's aging of the creation of the universe in only six yoms and the aging of humankind to be only six thousand years. The thought was, "How could this be possible?" The Bible was written long before modern scientific studies. Virtually nothing was known of the universe, the solar system, the earth, or the science of living organism at this time compared to our current scientific knowledge. Consider the improbability the Bible writers being able to accurately list the creation events and their chronological timing from the creation of the universe up to the creation of humankind. Now consider the description and order of events given in the Bible exactly fits the modern scientific understanding of both the creation of the physical and living world. There is no other book, or other writing in the world, even close to the jaw-dropping, awe-inspiring accuracy of information concerning the creation of the universe and living organisms on it than what was written in the Bible around thirty-five hundred years ago. Further, we now have scientific evidence and data to support that not only is the chronological roll out for the physical and living world correct, but six yoms and six thousand years are exactly on target. Coincidence?

Chapter 7

Old Testament–Era Evidence

4000 BC to 400 BC

Engineering requires an understanding of materials and chemistry. Along the way, the periodic table of elements becomes a familiar friend. At first, it may appear confusing and somewhat bewildering—rows and columns of abbreviated element names with numbers and information around them in each box. But upon study and training, the arrangement becomes clearer and the information becomes more understandable and useful.

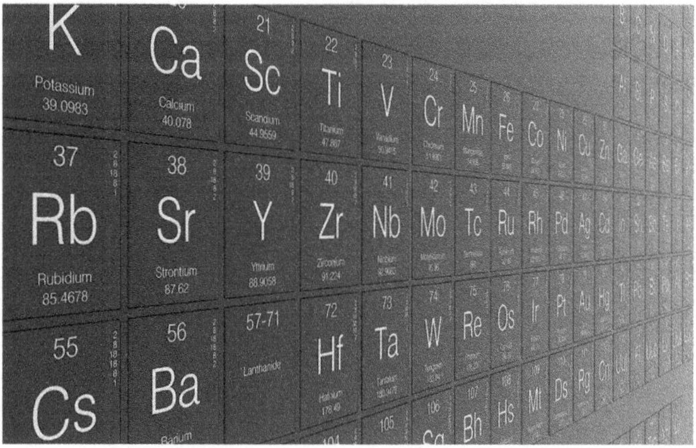

Figure 7.1: Periodic table of the elements

Such is the Old Testament. At first glance the Old Testament is a big, daunting compilation of books with a lot of information that may appear confusing and somewhat bewildering—books with people, places, and events of all different sorts. But like the periodical table of elements, upon formal study and training, the arrangement and the depth of the information becomes clearer and more insightful. In very brief summary, the Old Testament establishes the standard for living according to God's will. It points out sin in our lives or areas where we have not acted in accordance with God's will. Because of this, it points to the need for a savior, Jesus, to restore the broken relationship between us and God due to our sins.

So, in our march through time, we are ready to turn our attention to the time period between Adam and the birth of Jesus, approximately 4000 BC to 4 BC. Beyond the creation account given in the book of Genesis at the beginning of the Old Testament, this time period is what is covered in the Old Testament. As we walk through time, just a small portion of the archeological and factual evidence giving credence to the Bible's historical and geographical reliability will be pointed out. The Bible is not a history book, but it has a lot of history. Nor is it a science book, but it has a lot of science. The purpose of the Bible is to communicate God's will to us so we might understand him and his plan for our salvation through Jesus Christ. Archeology does not prove the divine nature of God, but it does prove the trustworthiness of the factual type information written in the Bible. Further, consider the fact that of the thousands and thousands of artifacts, historical documents, and relics that have been unearthed over the years, not one has contradicted any of the biblical writings.

The following chapter is not meant to be a play-by-play account of the Bible. Rather, it is a sampling through time of the people, places, and events as described by the Old Testament of the Bible and some of the evidence we have on these various descriptions so we can judge the overall trustworthiness of the Bible from a historical and geographical perspective.

We will continue our walk through time in chronological order, showing approximate dates for the various events per biblical dating. First, a portion of the biblical text will be given that talks about the person, place, or event, and then we will look at factual evidence supporting the biblical description.

4000 BC—Creation of Eve

Let's pick up where we last stopped on our timeline with the second human per the Bible, Eve:

> But for Adam no suitable helper was found. So the Lord God caused the man to fall into a deep sleep; and while he was sleeping, he took one of man's ribs and closed up the place with flesh. Then the Lord God made a woman from the rib he had taken out of the man, and he brought her to the man. (Genesis 2:20–22)
>
> Adam named his wife Eve, because she would become the mother of all the living. (Genesis 3:20)

The biblical account of the creation of Eve is rather simple and straightforward. But is there any factual evidence we can check to see if there is any trustworthiness in this account? In fact there is, and it comes from DNA. A man's rib contains both the male Y and the female X chromosome whereas a woman's rib contains only the female X chromosome. Since both X and Y chromosomes are necessary for human life, it is not possible to make a man from a woman's rib, but it is theoretically possible to create a woman from a man's rib.[1] So on this basis, the creation of Eve from Adam is plausible—keeping in mind, or course, with God all things are possible.

We also have results of human genome DNA studies involving diverse ethnic groups from around the world. The results of these studies indicate the entire world population did arise from one single mother, known as Mitochondrial Eve, or mtDNA Eve.[2] This is very significant. If evolution were true, then you would expect in various locations around the world multiple sets of human parents would have come into being. If so, then the human genomes would not trace back to a single female ancestor. Human genome studies indicating the human race traces back to a single female mother gives further credibility to the Bible. Multiple human genome studies examining the mutation rate, or genetic clock, concluding she lived six thousand years ago indicate not only is the Bible credible, it is right on target.

4000 BC—Garden of Eden

Turning now to where the original couple resided, the garden of Eden:

> Now the Lord God had planted a garden in the east, in Eden; and there he put the man he had formed. And the Lord God made all kinds of trees grow out of the ground—trees that were pleasing to the eye and good for food. In the middle of the garden were the tree of life and the tree of knowledge of good and evil. A river watering the garden flowed from Eden; from there it was separated into four headwaters. The name of the first is the Pishon; it winds through the entire land of Havilah, where there is gold. (The gold of that land is good; aromatic resin and onyx are also there.) The name of the second river is the Gihon; it winds through the entire land of Cush. The name of the third river is the Tigris; it runs along the east side of Asshur. And the fourth river is the Euphrates. (Genesis 2:8–14)

Ultimately, we cannot be certain of where the garden of Eden was located. We do know, however, the Tigris and Euphrates Rivers exist today. They flow from the region around Syria, through Iraq, and into the Persian Gulf. Whether or not these are the same rivers and location after the flood we cannot be certain. The flood and the draining water after the flood could have altered the landscape and therefore their course through the landscape.

Figure 7.2: Modern-day Euphrates River

4000 BC—Original Sin

This leads us to the biblical passage concerning the fall of humankind where Adam and Eve deliberately acted against the will of God while in the garden of Eden:

> And the Lord God commanded the man, "You are free to eat from any tree in the garden; but you must not eat from the tree of the knowledge of good and evil, for when you eat of it you will surely die." (Genesis 2:15–17)

> When the woman saw that the fruit of the tree was good for food and pleasing to the eye, and also

> desirable for gaining wisdom, she took some and ate it. She also gave some to her husband, who was with her, and he ate it. Then the eyes of both of them were opened, and they realized they were naked; so they sewed fig leaves together and made coverings for themselves. (Genesis 3:6–7)

God had instructed the couple to not eat from the tree of knowledge of good and evil. But after being tempted by Satan, they both chose to eat it and thus they sinned. Sin is anything that goes against God's will. God is a loving God, but he is also a just God. Per the Bible, God requires the shedding of blood for the remission of sins. Up until Jesus, animals were sacrificed for the temporary atonement, or covering over, of sin. However, Jesus himself became the once-and-for-all blood sacrifice for the sins of the world. Just as sin entered the world through one man, Adam, salvation entered the world through one man as well, Jesus.

Is there any archeological or scientific evidence of the original sin? No, not in a direct, measurable way, but in an indirect way, yes. The Bible teaches once sin entered the world through one man, Adam, all born after him had this intrinsic characteristic of being sinful by nature. We know from history and billions of people who have come after Adam that there has never been anyone who has lived a sinless life per God's standards as expressed in the Bible, except for Jesus. So although there is no direct, verifiable measurement that can be made of the original sin, we can see its consequences throughout history and to this day.

3500 BC—Tubal-Cain and the Bronze Age

Throughout the Bible there are short passages that are easy to read through and then easy to overlook. However, they contain real nuggets of truth and uphold the trustworthiness of the Bible. Such a passage involves a man named Tubal-Cain:

> Zilah also had a son, Tubal-Cain, who forged all kinds of tools out of bronze and iron. (Genesis 4:22)

This innocent-looking passage introduces us to Tubal-Cain, who forged tools out of bronze and iron. From dates and timing in the Bible, we know he lived around 3500 BC. This agrees well with the dating of the Bronze Age from bronze and iron artifacts unearthed through history.[3] Hence, the account checks out.

2348 BC—Noah and the Flood

Next, let's examine one of the most familiar accounts in the Bible to both believers and nonbelievers alike: Noah's ark and the flood:

> Now the earth was corrupt in God's sight and was full of violence. God saw how corrupt the earth had become, for all the people on earth had corrupted their ways. So God said to Noah, "I am going to put an end to all people, for the earth is filled with violence because of them. I am surely going to destroy both them and the earth. So make yourself an ark of cypress wood; make rooms in it and coat it with pitch inside and out. This is how you are to build it: the ark is to be 450 feet long, 75 feet wide and 45 feet high. Make a roof for it and finish the ark to within 18 inches of the top. Put a door in the side of the ark and make lower, middle and upper decks. I am going to bring floodwaters on the earth to destroy all life under the heavens, every creature that has the breath of life in it. Everything on earth will perish. But I will establish my covenant with you, and you will enter the ark—you and your sons and your wife and your sons' wives with you. You are to bring into the ark two of all living creatures, male and female, to keep them alive with you. Two

> of every kind of bird, of every kind of animal and of every kind of creature that moves along the ground will come to you to be kept alive. You are to take every kind of food that is to be eaten and store it away as food for you and for them. Noah did everything just as God commanded him. (Genesis 6:11–22)

The Bible explains the world had become so wicked, God decided to essentially wipe the slate clean with a flood, except for Noah and his family and representatives for each living creature. At first blush, this may seem like a mythological tall tale. But the evidence says otherwise. For instance, did you know, in addition to the Bible, there are many other worldwide accounts of a great flood that covered the earth dating back to the time of Noah?[4] The striking similarity of these accounts suggests these stories borrowed from the original biblical account.

One such artifact, the Gilgamesh Epic, are stone tablets found in Nineveh dating to 650 BC and currently housed in the British Museum in London. In it is a Babylonian account of a great flood that parallels many aspects of the biblical account.

In the 1990s, divers in the Black Sea (located between Russia and Turkey) discovered an old shoreline 450 feet below the current water level, indicating the lake had previously been 450 feet less deep. A global flood would have filled the basin, resulting in the much deeper lake level.[5] Fossil remains found in the soil date roughly to the time of the biblical flood. This evidence clearly supports a great flood.

Coal deposits throughout the world are another indication.[6] Coal comes from large masses of wood trapped under the pressure of sediment over long periods of time. Natural aging of forests does not produce the quantity of fallen trees needed all at once to produce coal deposits. Nor do dead, fallen trees come under the pressure of sedimentation that is necessary to turn them to coal since they would fall on the surface of the earth and simply decompose. It takes both large masses of dead trees and sedimentation such as that coming from settling flood waters to produce coal. Coal deposits support a great flood.

How about the ark itself? Is there any evidence of it? Actually yes!

> At the end of the hundred and fifty days the water had gone down, and on the seventeenth day of the seventh month the ark came to rest on the mountains of Ararat. (Genesis 8:3–4)

Mount Ararat is located in Turkey, and several expeditions have set out to find the ark. During WWII, spy planes flying over the mountain reported seeing a wooden vessel sitting high atop the mountain on an icy, snow-packed crag. Again in the 1950s and 1960s, military spy plane pilots allegedly saw and photographed an ark-like structure atop Mount Ararat. Since then, it is believed the ark has fallen further into the snow and ice pack and now lies beneath the surface. Several expeditions have set out to locate and bring back part of the ark from the mountaintop. There have been a multitude of reports and disputes concerning the evidence found. In their book *In Search of Noah's Ark*, Dave Balsinger and Charles Sellier list the undisputed facts concerning the ark:[7]

1. At about the fourteen-thousand-foot level on Mount Ararat in Turkey, there is a very large wooden boat-like structure buried beneath many feet of ice and snow.
2. A boat-like structure has been mentioned as being on Mount Ararat by explorers and historians of several civilizations beginning as early as 700 BC.
3. During the 1800s, this structure was observed by many local explorers, including numerous Turkish military authorities, who gave the structure official government recognition in the news media.

4. In 1955, a filmed expedition recovered wood from the structure nearly thirty-five feet below the surface of an ice pack.
5. The recovered wood, subjected to numerous types of dating tests, revealed an age range from twelve hundred to five thousand years old.
6. Early in the 1970s, American spy planes and weather and military satellites photographed the structure on Mount Ararat.
7. The only specific historical source that can be used to possibly identify this artifact is found in the biblical book of Genesis, which mentions the ancient landing of a large boat "on the mountains of Ararat."

Figure 7.3: Mount Ararat in Turkey

Yet another source of evidence comes from an unlikely source, the Human Genome Project. As previously discussed, the goal of this project was to map the human DNA genome for the purpose of medical advancement and treatment of various illnesses and diseases. Somewhat unexpectedly, implications and evidence concerning the origins of humankind regarding creationism versus evolution have surfaced. Support of the global flood is one of them.

First, results of various human genome studies indicate there was a "human population bottleneck" less than ten thousand years ago. Second, the worldwide DNA tree and mitochondrial clock point to a recent (six thousand years ago) sole female ancestor, mitochondrial Eve, from whom the entire human population descended.[8] Third, in 2016, Dr. Nathaniel Jeanson published results from his worldwide mtDNA studies indicating there are three main branches to the female lineage, and all three are very similar, indicating a very recent divergence from a single female ancestor.[9]

A worldwide flood, as recorded in the Bible, fits this evidence quite well. First, the timing of the flood aligns with this study's conclusion of a population bottleneck several thousands of years ago, and less than ten thousand years. Second, there were eight people on Noah's ark, Noah and his wife, his three sons, and their wives. A population bottleneck! Next, the three branches of the female lineage aligns exactly with the three wives of Noah's sons. Per the Bible, Noah and his wife did not have more children once the ark came to rest on dry ground. Only his sons and their wives had children. Finally, per the Bible the three wives of Noah's sons would have been the tenth-generation descendants of Eve, and therefore shared a recent common ancestry from a single female ancestor. The match is remarkable.

So, the global flood and Noah's ark that may have appeared to be a tall mythological tale at one time is now supported by multiple scientifically verifiable findings and evidence.

2247 BC—Tower of Babel

Another short passage in the Bible with real, interesting authenticity implications for the Bible involves the tower of Babel:

> Now the whole world had one language and a common speech. (Genesis 11:1)

> Then they said, "Come, let us build ourselves a city, with a tower that reaches to the heavens. (Genesis 11:4)

> The Lord said, "If as one people speaking the same language they have begun to do this, then nothing they plan to do will be impossible for them. Come, let us go down and confuse their language so they will not understand each other. So the Lord scattered them from there over all the earth, and they stopped building the city. That is why it was called Babel—because there the Lord confused the language of the whole world. From there the Lord scattered them over the face of the whole earth. (Genesis 11:6–9)

Compelling evidence has recently surfaced inscribed on the face of a clay tablet dating to 600 BC, originally found more than one hundred years ago, and now belonging to the private collection of Norwegian businessman Martin Schoyen.[10] Inscribed on this tablet is a graphic depiction of the Tower of Babel along with a written description. The Tower of Babel was a seven-tiered ziggurat and located in the ancient city of Babylon. The ruins and rubble of the once-mighty tower have been located in what is now modern-day Iraq.

Figure 7.4: Clay tablet dating to 600 BC depicting Tower of Babel (used with permission: The Schoyan Collection, MS 2063)

Additionally, there is evidence the world did speak one language in ancient times. There are written accounts from ancient Sumeria, Burma, and India all indicating at one time there was one language in the world. Secular linguists are also puzzled by the diversity of languages that are not genetically related. If evolution were true, linguists would expect language itself to also evolve over time. But the unrelated languages around the world argue against this. However, the description given in the Bible of God creating diversity in the languages at the tower of Babel completely answers this problem.

1921 BC—Call of Abraham

Abraham was from the city of Ur and was to become the father of the nation of Israel:

> Terah took his son Abram, his grandson Lot son of Haran, and his daughter-in-law Sarai, the wife of his son Abram, and together they set out from Ur of the Caldeans to go to Canaan. But when they came to Haran, they settled there. (Genesis 11:31–32)
>
> The Lord had said to Abram, "Leave your country your people and your father's household and go to the land I will show you. I will make you into a great nation and I will bless you; I will make your name great and you will be a blessing. I will bless those who bless you, and whoever curses you I will curse; and all peoples on earth will be blessed through you." (Genesis 12:1–3)

Abram, the first Hebrew, who later became known as Abraham, was called by God to leave his home and to go to a place specified by God. The word *Hebrew* means to pass or cross over, which is what Abram did in traveling from his home to the new land. The ancient city Abraham was from, the Ur of the Chaldeans located in southern Iraq, has been located and excavated by archeologists.[11]

Abraham was a man of great faith, and God promised him a great nation would come from him and that all people on earth would be blessed through him. Abraham became the father of Isaac, Isaac the father of Jacob, and Jacob (who is also known as Israel—hence the name of the Jewish nation) the father of twelve sons, which became the twelve tribes and nation of Israel, which still exists today. Thus God fulfilled his promise that a great nation would come from him. Further, Jesus Christ is a descendent of Abraham since both Mary and Joseph were descendants of Abraham, as will be seen in a later chapter. Therefore, God also fulfilled his promise to Abraham that all people on earth would be blessed through him.

Figure 7.5: Restored bottom stories of a ziggurat from Abraham's hometown of Ur

1898 BC—Covenant of Circumcision

This is another one of those nuggets inside the Bible that is very easy to overlook without some thought and examination. It involves the ideal date for performing circumcision:

> For the generations to come every male among you who is eight days old must be circumcised,

> including those born in your household or bought with money from a foreigner—those who are not your offspring. Whether born in your household or bought with your money, they must be circumcised. My covenant in your flesh is to be an everlasting covenant. (Genesis 17:12–13)

This topic can evoke snickers among even the most straight-faced of people, but there actually is some interesting evidence of divine influence on this topic. Modern medical studies have shown the eighth day is the optimal day to perform circumcision to minimize medical risks.[12] Moses wrote this passage in 1455 BC, long before any depth to medical practices or the human body were known. He could have picked the second day, the third month, or even the fourth year. How would Moses have known to specify the eighth day unless he was in fact guided by divine influence?

1900 BC—Hittite Nation

> So I have come down to rescue them from the hand of the Egyptians and to bring them up out of that land into a good and spacious land, a land flowing with milk and honey—the home of the Canaanites, Hittites, Amorites, Perizzites, Hivites and Jebusites. (Exodus 3:8)

Throughout the Old Testament of the Bible, the mighty Hittite empire is mentioned. But up until the 1900s, no other information was found on the Hittites. Many Bible scoffers pointed to this and criticized the reliability of the Bible. Then in 1906 in northeast Turkey, clay tablets were found in Hattusa, the large capital city of the Hittite nation. It is located about ninety miles east of Ankara, Turkey. Although the ruins of the massive, sprawling city were known for years, researchers did not realize this was home to the Hittites. Over thirty-five thousand clay tablets have been unearthed since this time describing the Hittite nation exactly as the Bible had described several thousands of years earlier.[13]

Figure 7.6: Gate of Hattusa, the Hittite capital

1600 BC—Israelite Slaves in Egypt

Driven by widespread famine, the nation of Israel moved into Egypt and lived among the Egyptians, who had the foresight to store up food. After a period of time, and with a new pharaoh over Egypt, the Jews were put into slavery for the Egyptians:

> So they put slave masters over them to oppress them with forced labor, and they built Pithom and Rameses as store cities for Pharaoh. But the more they were oppressed, the more they multiplied and spread; so the Egyptians came to dread the Israelites and worked them ruthlessly. They made their lives bitter with hard labor in brick and mortar and with all kinds of work in the fields; in all their hard labor the Egyptians used them ruthlessly. (Exodus 1:11–14)

Due to a series of events and an extended famine and drought in their country, the sons of Jacob (Israel) ended up in Egypt. Ironically,

Egypt's wise action to store up grain in years of bounty was due to the vision of Jacob's youngest son, Joseph. The older brothers, driven by their jealousy and desire to get rid of him, had sold Joseph into slavery to the Egyptians. At first, the Egyptians and Pharaoh were friendly and cordial toward the Israelites, primarily due to Joseph, who was viewed very favorably. However, with the death of this pharaoh, the next pharaoh taking his place cast a suspicious eye toward the Israelites, and they were put into forced labor.

A number of artifacts have been found from this era, including structures built with chopped straw and mud from the Nile River. The last of the great pyramids found south of modern-day Cairo, near the ancient city Hawara, is one such structure. It was built by Pharaoh Amenemhet III, who could possibly be the pharaoh whose daughter adopted the Hebrew baby Moses.[14]

Figure 7.7: Ancient mud-brick pyramid at Hawara built by Pharaoh Amenemhet III

1571 BC—Birth of Moses

After the Israelites spent hundreds of years of being slaves and oppressed in Egypt, God heard their plea and raised one of them, Moses, to lead them out of Egypt. Because the Israelites had become very populous, the pharaoh instructed the Egyptians to kill all newborn male Hebrew babies by throwing them into the Nile River. Moses's mother managed to hide him from the Egyptians for the first three months of his life. When she realized she could no longer hide him, she placed him in a basket among the reeds in the Nile River. The pharaoh's own daughter discovered Moses in the reeds and raised him, even having Moses's biological mother nurse him. So Moses, a Hebrew and Israelite, grew up in the Egyptian pharaoh's palace. There he received the finest education and training available throughout the land.

Although there are no known direct artifacts or archeological evidence of Moses's existence dating from this time, such as an engraved rock or statue, there actually is a huge amount of evidence in the Bible itself. You see, Moses is credited with writing the first five books of the Bible: Genesis, Exodus, Leviticus, Numbers, and Deuteronomy. It was his education and training received in the pharaoh's palace that enabled him to write at a time when it was very uncommon to be literate. Coincidence?

1491 BC—Exodus from Egypt and the Passover Meal

Perhaps you have seen the Charlton Heston movie where he plays the role of Moses leading the Jews out of bondage in Egypt. The proverbial straw that broke the camel's back, or in this case the pharaoh's heart, and caused him to tell the Jews to leave his land was the plague of the firstborn God cast down on the people. This also led to the institution of the Passover meal among the Jews:

> The Lord said to Moses and Aaron in Egypt … "On that same night I will pass through Egypt and strike down every firstborn—both men and animals—and I will bring judgment on all the gods of Egypt. I am the Lord. The blood will be a sign for you on the houses where you are: and when I see the blood, I will pass over you. No destructive plague will touch you when I strike Egypt." (Exodus 12:1, 12–13)

There are no known artifacts of the exodus of the Israelites from Egypt. God had struck the pharaoh and the Egyptians with a series of plagues, but the pharaoh's heart was hardened and he would not allow the Jews to leave. The final plague, however, changed the pharaoh's mind, and the Israelites were told to leave. As described above, the book of Exodus describes the plague of the firstborn. The Hebrews were to take a blemish-free lamb and sacrifice it. The blood was to be sprinkled on the sides and tops of the doorframes of the dwellings where they would eat the roasted lamb that night. During the night, God would pass through Egypt and strike down every firstborn, except for the houses where the blood of the lamb was on the doorframe. This became the Passover feast Jesus was celebrating the night before his crucifixion. When Jesus is referred to as the Lamb of God, it is this sacrificial blemish-free lamb from the Passover feast serving as a symbol of what Jesus represents. Those accepting Jesus as the Christ in faith are extended eternal grace by God through the blood Jesus shed on the cross as an atoning sacrifice for our sins. This Passover meal was a central part to the Jewish faith and was practiced by the early Christians, and it still is the highest point during a Christian worship service, lends credibility to its original occurrence.

Figure 7.8: Christian communion meal

1491 BC—The Ten Commandments

After leaving Egypt and heading to the Promised Land, God led the nation of Israel to the foot of Mount Sinai, a place you can go to today, and called Moses up the mountain:

> The Lord descended to the top of Mount Sinai and called Moses to the top of the mountain. (Exodus 19:20)

There on Mount Sinai, God etched in stone tablets the Ten Commandments for Moses and his people. The Ten Commandments were put in the ark of the covenant, and then placed in the innermost part of their worship tent, the holy of holies. When the temple was built in Jerusalem by Solomon, the ark of the covenant and the Ten Commandments were put inside the holy of holies portion of the temple. In 587 BC when the Babylonians destroyed Jerusalem, there is no definitive record of what became of the ark. However, the Bible indicates it will be in heaven.

The Old Testament law, or the Mosaic Law, as it is often referred to, was given to the Jews by God through Moses following this series of events at Mount Sinai. The Mosaic Law consisted of the Ten Commandments, hundreds of ordinances or specific laws, and the worship system. The purpose of the law was primarily to reveal God's holy character and his will to the people, as well as to reveal the sinfulness of people.

Figure 7.9: Mount Sinai

1491 BC—Israel Wandering in the Desert

Though God had done miraculous deeds right before the Israelites' eyes in leading them out of Egypt and providing for them as they traveled toward the Promised Land, they quickly became disobedient and sinned against God:

> The Lord's anger burned against Israel and he made them wander in the desert forty years, until the whole generation of those who had done evil in his site were gone. (Numbers 32:13)

The Promised Land the nation of Israel was traveling to is only 260 straight-line miles from Egypt. This is less than one month's walk from Egypt. However, the Bible teaches us due to their grumblings and disobedience, God allowed them to wander in the desert between the two places for forty years. The Sinai Desert is another real location discussed in the Bible that you can visit today.

Figure 7.10: Sinai Desert

1451 BC—Israelites Enter the Promised Land

At the end of the forty years when the whole generation who had turned from God had passed, including Moses, Joshua led them across the Jordan River and into the Promised Land:

> When the whole nation had finished crossing the Jordan, the Lord said to Joshua, "Choose twelve men from among the people, one from each tribe, and tell them to take up twelve stones from the middle of the Jordan from right where the priests stood and to carry them over with you and put them down at the place where you stay tonight." (Joshua 4:1–3)

The nation of Israel entered the Promised Land from the east by crossing over the Jordan River. There they would fight against many other nations for control of the land. The nation of Israel lived there until the Assyrian and Babylonian defeat and captivity beginning in 722 BC and 586 BC respectively.

One proof of Israelites in the Promised Land comes from an

engraved stone discovered, called the Merenptah Stele, standing over seven feet tall and carved into a tombstone-like shape.[15] The hieroglyphic text contains the earliest mention of the name *Israel* outside of the Bible. Text engraved on the stone states "Israel" was living in the Promised Land in 1230 BC. This artifact is housed in the Egyptian Museum in Cairo.

1400 BC—Battle of Jericho

In their pursuit to take over the Promised Land, Israel came up against one of the oldest-known cities in the world, Jericho:

> When the trumpets sounded, the people shouted, and at the sound of the trumpet, when the people gave a loud shout, the wall collapsed; so every man charged straight in, and they took the city. (Joshua 6:20)
>
> Then they burned the whole city and everything in it. (Joshua 6:24)

One of the most famous battles, and earliest battle taking place as the Israelites entered the Promised Land, occurred at Jericho. The Bible describes how the fortifying walls around the city collapsed supernaturally and the Israelites were able to charge straight in, take the city, and then burn it.

The city of Jericho has been found by archeologists, excavated, and studied in great detail.[16] The dating of the destruction of Jericho has been confirmed to be around 1400 BC. The remains indicate the fortifying walls of the city collapsed and were not broken down from the outside. When the walls collapsed, they fell outward and not inward. This created a natural ramp for the Israelites to attack straight into the city as the Bible states. Next, destruction by fire is evident in the charred remains and smoke deposits on the walls. The smoke residue also indicates the fires occurred after the walls fell down, not before, also in agreement with the Bible. Finally, there are large amounts of burnt grain in the ruins. At this time grain was a precious commodity. Why would attacking forces not keep the grain as part of the loot? Again, the Bible provides the answers as it tells us the Israelites were instructed by God to not keep anything from the city.

Figure 7.11: Ancient ruins from the city of Jericho

1245 BC—Canaanites

The Canaanites were another of Israel's frequently mentioned foes in the Bible:

> After the death of Joshua, the Israelites asked the Lord, "Who will be the first to go up and fight for us against the Canaanites?" (Judges 1:1)

The Canaanites lived in the Promised Land during this period, and Israel fought against them to drive them out of the land. The Canaanites were known for idol worship, particularly the idol gods of Baal and Asherah. The people of Israel are warned to worship the true God and to keep away from idol worship. Hundreds of clay tablets with accounts of Canaanite gods and goddesses have been found in the ancient city of Ugarit in modern-day Syria, as well as plaques and images of their idols confirming the biblical description.[17] One such artifact, a large stone tablet with an image of the storm God Baal holding a thunderbolt, is housed in the Louvre Museum in Paris, France.

1150 BC—Israelite City of Dan

Speaking of Canaanites, the city of Dan was originally inhabited by Canaanites until it was conquered by Israel around 1150 BC:[18]

> The city was in a valley near Beth Rehob. The Danites rebuilt the city and settled there. They named it Dan after their forefather Dan, who was born to Israel—though the city used to be called Laish. (Judges 18:28–29)
>
> After seeking advice, the king made two golden calves. He said to the people, "It is too much for you to go up to Jerusalem. Here are your gods, O Israel, who brought you up out of Egypt." One he set up in Bethel, and the other in Dan. And this thing became a sin; the people went even as far as Dan to worship the one there. Jeroboam built shrines on high places and appointed priests from all sorts of people, even though they were not Levites. (1 Kings 12:28–31)

Dan became Israel's northernmost city. Numerous biblical artifacts have been found in the ancient city of Dan by archeologists confirming its existence and exact location. Even the high place where Jeroboam placed the golden calves has been found in Dan.[19]

Figure 7.12: Ancient Tel Dan wall

1060 BC—Philistines

Yet another one of Israel's enemies was the Philistines. The short-lived battle between David, who would later become Israel's king, and Goliath the Philistine is epic and well known:

> Now the Philistines gathered their forces for war and assembled at Socoh in Judah. (1 Samuel 17:1)
>
> A champion named Goliath, who was from Garth, came out of the Philistine camp. He was over nine feet tall. (1 Samuel 17:4)

The Philistines were one of the main nemeses of Israel in the Promised Land. The Philistines are mentioned several hundred times in the Old Testament. Israel fought against them from Samson to King David, who fought against, and killed, Goliath when he was a young boy. The earliest known artifact of the Philistines is carved on a wall of an Egyptian temple at Thebes that dates from around 1160 BC. In the wall carving, the Philistines are depicted in battle and listed by name.

Recently an ancient Philistine cemetery containing more than 211 individuals and dating from the eleventh to the eighth century

BC was discovered outside the walls of ancient Ashkelon, a major Philistine city.[20] Future studies of these skeletons should provide further insight into the Philistines.

Figure 7.13: Valley of Elah where David killed Goliath

1055 BC—King David

King David is perhaps Israel's most renowned king and one of the most important figures in Jewish history:

> When all the elders of Israel had come to King David in Hebron, they made a compact with them at Hebron before the Lord, and they anointed David king over Israel. David was thirty years old when he became king, and he reigned forty years. (2 Samuel 5:3–4)

Even though David is a prominent figure in the Bible, no artifacts outside of the Bible had been found of him for years. Then in 1993, an archeologist in the ancient Israelite city of Dan found an inscribed stone referencing David.[21] The Aramaic expression reads "the house of David" and the "king of Israel." This artifact, known as the Tel Dan Stele, is housed in the Israel Museum in Jerusalem.

1040 BC—Pool of Gibeon

The Pool of Gibeon is a man-made structure King David and others visited that still exists today:

> Abner son of Ner, together with the men of Ish-Bosheth son of Saul, left Mahanaim and went to Gibeon. Joab son of Zeruiah and David's men went out and met them at the pool of Gibeon. One group sat down on one side of the pool and one group on the other side. (2 Samuel 2:12–13)

The pool of Gibeon, built before 1000 BC, was found in 1956 in Gibeon, six miles north of Jerusalem.[22] It goes down eighty feet and is fed by a spring outside of the city by a hand-dug tunnel. This protected water supply fed into the city for strategic defense purposes. The size of this tunnel and pool is immense. It would be easy to write off the account of the pool and tunnel as a fabricated story of the Bible. But discovery of its actual presence and being able to see its magnitude lends credibility to the reliability of the Bible.

1000 BC—Israelite City of Gezer

There are many cities and towns mentioned in the Bible. Some, like Jerusalem, are still bustling cities today. Others, like Gezer, are desolate but have been excavated by archeologists and conform to their biblical descriptions:

> Pharaoh King of Egypt had attacked and captured Gezer. He had set it on fire. He killed its Canaanite inhabitants and then gave it as a wedding gift to his daughter, Solomon's wife. And Solomon rebuilt Gezer. (1 Kings 9:16–17)

The gateway of Gezer is very similar to those found at the city of Megiddo and Hazor that were also built by King Solomon substantiating the biblical passage.[23] Evidence of destruction as described in the Bible is also visible.

Figure 7.14: Ruins from six-chambered gate at Hazor

950 BC—Israelite City of Beersheba

Beersheba is yet another city in the Promised Land referred to in the Bible that archeologists have located and excavated. The evidence found supports the accuracy of the historical, geographical, and narrative descriptions given in the Bible.[24]

> During Solomon's lifetime Judah and Israel, from Dan to Beersheba, lived in safety, each man under his own vine and fig tree. (1 Kings 4:25)

Whereas Dan was Israel's key fortress city to the north, Beersheba was a fortress city to the south. The excavated strong walls and gates of Beersheba support its biblical description.

Figure 7.15: Tel Beersheba ancient ruins

850 BC—Moabite King Mesha

Bible accounts of non-Jewish people and places such as King Mesha have also been confirmed through archeological finds:

> Now Mesha king of Moab raised sheep, and he had to supply the king of Israel with a hundred thousand lambs and with the wool of a hundred thousand rams. (2 Kings 3:4)

In 1868 a three-foot carved stone slab, now known as the Moabite Stone, was found east of the Dead Sea. One of the accounts on the stone slab was of King Mesha from Moab from around 850 BC, the same Mesha mentioned in the Bible.[25] This artifact, also known as the Mesha Stele, is housed in the Louvre Museum in Paris, France.

Figure 7.16: Replica of Moabite stone

841 BC—Israelite King Jehu and Assyrian King Shalmaneser
King Jehu was a godly king of Israel in the northern kingdom of Israel who eliminated Baal worship (idol worship). But his reign began a decline in the Israelites' fortunes. Shortly after King Jehu took the throne, Assyrian King Shalmaneser mounted an offensive against neighboring kings, including King Jehu's northern kingdom.

> Jehu got up and went into the house. Then the prophet poured the oil on Jehu's head and declared, "This is what the Lord, the God of Israel, says: 'I anoint you king over the Lord's people Israel.'" (2 Kings 9:6)

In 1846 the Black Obelisk was found in the palace at Nimrod. It is a four-sided black stone pillar over six feet tall with drawings and writings inscribed on it. It shows Jehu, the king of Israel, bowing down to the Assyrian king, Shalmaneser.[26] The large artifact is currently on display at the British Museum in London.

758 BC—Israelite King Uzziah

Another king in the long line of Israel's kings described in the Bible is King Uzziah:

> The other events of Uzziah's reign, from beginning to end, are recorded by the prophet Isaiah son of Amoz. Uzziah rested with his fathers and was buried near them in a field for burial that belonged to the kings, for people said, "He had leprosy." (2 Chronicles 26:22–23)

King Uzziah ruled Judah (at this time Israel was split into two regions, Israel to the North and Judah to the South) from 792 to 740 BC. A stone plaque was found outside a Russian church on the Mount of Olives outside Jerusalem that states, "Here, the bones of Uzziah, King of Judah, were brought. Do not open."[27] The plaque is part of the Israel Museum collection in Jerusalem.

710 BC—Siloam tunnel in Jerusalem

Another place that is described in the Bible and can be visited today is the Siloam tunnel:

> As for the other events in Hezekiah's reign, all his achievements and how he made the pool and the tunnel by which he brought water into the city. (2 Kings 20:20)

In 1880, a carved stone was found along the wall of the Siloam tunnel described in the Bible above. The inscription on the stone celebrates the completion of this tunnel.[28]

Figure 7.17: Carved stone with inscription found along Siloam tunnel dating to 701 BC

586 BC—Babylon the Great

Nebuchadnezzar was the Assyrian king of the powerful Babylonian Empire who defeated the Israelites. He destroyed the temple in Jerusalem built by King Solomon, looted the Israelite possessions and people and took them back to Babylon:

> As the Lord had declared, Nebuchadnezzar removed all the treasures from the temple of the Lord and from the royal palace, and took away all the gold articles that Solomon king of Israel had made for the temple of the Lord. He carried into exile all Jerusalem; all the officers and fighting men, and all the craftsmen and artisans—a total of ten thousand. Only the poorest people of the land were left. (2 Kings 24:13–14)

Archeologists have found a Babylonian chronicle etched on a stone telling of the capture of Jerusalem on March 16, 597 BC, by Nebuchadnezzar.[29]

Babylon was once a mighty city. It is located fifty-six miles south of modern-day Baghdad and covered several thousand acres.[30] Here the palace of King Nebuchadnezzar was found and excavated. Among its ruins is a ziggurat, which is a pyramid shaped, stair-stepped tower.

However, per the Bible, the mighty, powerful, and splendid Babylon was prophesied to suffer the wrath of God:

> Babylon, the jewel of kingdoms, the glory of the Babylonian's pride, will be overthrown by God like Sodom and Gomorrah. She will never be inhabited or lived in through all generations; no Arab will pitch his tent there, no shepherd will rest his flocks there. (Isaiah 13:19–20)

Any guesses what the ancient city of Babylon is like today? It is exactly as Isaiah prophesied hundreds of years before its demise: desolate.

Figure 7.18: Desolate ruins from ancient Babylon

539 BC—Persian King Cyrus Decree

It was King Cyrus of Persia (modern-day Iran) who took Babylon in 539 BC. After his victory, he issued a decree that the Jews held in captivity in Babylon would be freed and allowed to go back to their native land to rebuild:

> Who says of Cyrus, "He is my shepherd and will accomplish all that I please; he will say of Jerusalem, 'Let it be rebuilt,' and of the temple, 'Let its foundation be laid.'" (Isaiah 44:28)

The prophet Isaiah wrote these words around 690 BC, 154 years before the actual decree by King Cyrus of Persia (modern-day Iran) in 536 BC.[31]

A small clay cylinder, resembling an ear of corn in appearance, was found at ancient Babylon describing King Cyrus of Persia's defeat of Babylon and his decree to let the Israelite captives free to return to their land and rebuild their temples, exactly as described in the Bible. The inscription on the cylinder dates to 539 BC and is housed in the British Museum in London.

536 BC—Return Home

Following years of captivity in Assyria and Babylon, the Israelites were freed and allowed to go back to their native lands and rebuild, which they did.

435 BC—Silent Years

From the close of the book of Malachi until the time of Jesus's arrival on earth, there are no new biblical writings. The Bible is silent during this period. But the stage is set. God had given his law and commands to the people, yet no one was able to completely fulfill them. The people went through periods of time of turning toward God and life got better, followed by periods of time where they turned away from God, and disaster ensued. This set the stage for God to send the Savior into the world, Jesus.

Summary

This chapter is just a sliver of the archeological evidence supporting the Bible and Christian faith. Thousands of Old Testament–era artifacts have been unearthed, and scientific discoveries again and again confirm the reliability of the Bible when it describes people, places, and events. Some of these accounts, such as Noah's ark and the flood, seem outlandish, but in fact, are supported with factual evidence. Some of the evidence, such as the recent Human Genome Project, is still being fully flushed out on its implications concerning the creation of life and the reliability of the Bible. But it is already putting solid, credible evidence in favor of the Bible and the Christian faith. And as time goes on, the evidence keeps piling up in favor of the Christian faith. Coincidence?

Chapter 8

Prophecies on Jesus

4000 BC to 400 BC

One of the existential pleasures of engineering is being able to predict physical behavior ahead of time, make prototype parts, and then test those parts and see the behavior occur as predicted. Whether it be an electromagnetic machine design, a thermal system, fluid flow, an electrical circuit, or a structural element, it is very satisfying to predict performance and then see it materialize with actual test data as predicted.

Even though there are engineering marvels, these types of engineering predictions involve observed physical laws remaining constant over time. There is nothing supernatural or unexplainable in the observed behavior of the system. This is because they do not involve unpredictable factors such as human thought and emotions. As we will see in this chapter, engineering predictions are mere child's play at best compared to the predictions in the Bible. The Bible is full of predictions on people, places, and events and in particular, Jesus. The predictions concerning Jesus are astounding.

So why the big deal over Jesus? If you have little or no knowledge or understanding of Jesus, you must be wondering at this point who he is, what he did, and why he is so important, or even more basic, did he even exist at all?

Jesus is the centerpiece of the Christian faith. But he is much more than that. Jesus is God. God took on flesh and blood to become human like us. He did not just come to the earth and live thirty-three years to be crucified, resurrect from the dead, and then ascend into heaven never to be seen or heard from again. Jesus being God, has always existed and is the creator of the universe as we already examined. He is as alive today as he was before the beginning of time.

So why did the all-powerful, all-knowing, everlasting God humble himself and become man in the personage of Jesus? The answer is simple: love. God loves us. God loves all of His creation. But for free will to even exist, there must also be justice. No justice, no free will. If our actions have no right and wrong associated with them and no justice for wrong actions, there really is not free will because our choices do not matter. But God has given us free will. We are not preprogrammed robots designed to worship God, but rather we are free to choose what we do and say. However sometimes we do things against God's will and anything going against God's will is sin. For free will to exist, God cannot allow sin to go unpunished. It is the price we pay for the luxury of having free will. God requires the shedding of blood for the atonement or covering over of sin. Jesus came into the world and lived a perfect, sinless life to become the once-and-forever sacrifice on the cross for the redemption of our sins. God's plan is very simple: turn away from our sins, accept in faith Jesus is the Christ, which is to say the savior, and God will forgive our sins, both now and for eternity. The sacrificial blood of Jesus on the cross will atone for, or cover over, our sins. So God became man in the form of Jesus, out of love for us, so our sins can be forgiven and ultimately we can live with him in heaven for eternity.

So how do we go about providing evidence to back up these bold statements? God becoming man—show me the proof on that one! Well, the answer in part is we already have, or at least the start of the foundation with our look at the Bible. We have started from the beginning of time and walked through time showing how the Bible is trustworthy from a historical, geographical and scientific perspective concerning the origin of the universe and the origin of humankind. Just the first thirty-one verses in the Bible (Genesis 1:1–31) set it apart from any other writing in the world. It was written thirty-five hundred years ago, and it is amazing the scientific insight and accuracy with which it was written. This alone should raise your eyebrows regarding divine influence on the Bible. But is there more? Is there more evidence of divine influence on the Christian faith that would lead to an intelligence-based decision to put your faith in Jesus? There sure is—prophecies! For those for whom evidence of the divine is a stumbling block on their way to faith, God has given us fulfilled prophecies in the Bible we can examine and be assured of his divine influence.

There are well over one thousand prophecies throughout the Bible about people, cities, and nations, most of which are already fulfilled. By one count there are 1,239 prophecies in the Old Testament and 578 prophecies in the New Testament, for a total of 1,817 prophecies.[1] Before we focus in on Jesus, take a look at just a few of the fulfilled prophecies on people, the city of Jerusalem, and the nation of Israel.

Prophecies on People		
Prophecy	Description	Fulfillment
Numbers 14:24, 30	Joshua and Caleb to enter Canaan after forty years	Joshua 3:7, 17; 14:6–12
Jeremiah 43:9–13, 46:26, Ezekiel 29:19–20	Nebuchadnezzar to invade Egypt	Testimony in history
Isaiah 44:28	Cyrus to allow Jews to go back and rebuild Jerusalem	Ezra 1:1–2
Daniel 2:32–39; 7:6; 8:5–8, 21; 11:3	Alexander the Great to conquer Greece and establish a world empire	Testimony in history
Daniel 8:5–8	Alexander to defeat the Persians	Testimony in history
Daniel 8:8, 22, 11:4	Alexander to die suddenly and his kingdom to be divided into four parts	Testimony in history
Isaiah 40:3–5, Malachi 3:1, Luke 1:76–77	John the Baptist to be Jesus's forerunner	Matthew 3:1–11, Luke 3:2–6
John 21:18–19, 2 Peter 1:12–14	Peter to suffer martyrdom for Jesus	Testimony in history
Act 9:16	Paul to suffer much for Jesus	2 Corinthians 11:23–28, 12:7–10, Galatians 6:17

Prophecies on Jerusalem		
Prophecy	Description	Fulfillment
Deuteronomy 12:5–6, 11, Joshua 9:27, 10:1, 1 Kings 8:29, 11:36, 15:4	Jerusalem to be God's chosen place	Testimony in history
1 Kings 9:7–9, Psalm 79:1, Jeremiah 7:11–14; 26:18	Solomon's temple to be destroyed	2 Chronicles 36:19 Lamentations 7
Isaiah 44:28	Jerusalem to be rebuilt after Jews spend seventy years in Babylonian captivity	Ezra 1:1-4
Daniel 9:25–26	The walls to be rebuilt 483 years prior to the coming of Jesus	Testimony in history
Luke 21:24	To be trampled upon by the Gentiles until the Second Coming	Testimony in history

Prophecies on Israel		
Prophecy	Description	Fulfillment
Genesis 9:26	The people of Shem to be especially blessed by God	John 4:22
Genesis 12:2	A great nation to come from Abraham	Numbers 23:10
Genesis 15:13	Egypt to host Israel for 400 years and afflict them	Exodus 12:40, Acts 7:6
Jeremiah 31:35–37	The nation of Israel to exist forever	Testimony in history
Deuteronomy 28:65–67	Israel to become a byword among the nations	Testimony in history
Isaiah 53:1-9	Israel to reject her Messiah	Luke 23:13–25
Deuteronomy 30:3; Ezekiel 36:24, 37:1–14	Israel to return to Palestine in the latter days prior to the Second Coming of Jesus	Testimony of history since 1948

Now let's turn to Jesus. So how many prophecies are there on just Jesus alone? By one count, there are 353 prophecies on Jesus alone.[2] Admittedly, at first glance most of the three hundred–plus prophecies concerning Jesus are not lengthy or overly detailed, but some are. But taken as a whole, they become like a giant connect-the-dots picture. Jesus clearly and unmistakably emerges as the prophesied Christ or Savior of the world when these prophecies are viewed collectively.

The following is just an abbreviated list of the three hundred–plus prophecies on Jesus contained in the Old Testament of the Bible.

Prophecies about Jesus		
Prophecy	Description	Fulfillment
Genesis 3:15	He would be born of a woman.	Galatians 4:4
Genesis 12:3, 7; 17:7 1400 BC	He would be from the line of Abraham.	Romans 9:5 Galatians 3:16 AD 48
Genesis 49:10	He would be from the tribe of Judah.	Hebrew 7:14 Revelation 5:5
Micah 5:2 800–700 BC	He would come from Bethlehem.	Luke 2:4-7 AD 60
Isaiah 7:14 800–700 BC	He would be born from a virgin, and his name would mean "God with us"— Immanuel.	Matthew 1:18–25 AD 50
2 Samuel 7:12–13	He would be from the house of David.	Luke 1:31–33 Romans 1:3
2 Samuel 7:11–12 Psalm 132:11 Jeremiah 23:5	He would be given the throne of David.	Luke 1:31–32
Daniel 2:44, 7:14 Micah 4:7	His throne would be eternal.	Luke 1:33
Isaiah 40:3–5 Malachi 3:1	He would have a forerunner.	Matthew 3:1–3 Luke 1:76–78, 3:3–6
Psalm 72:10 Isaiah 60:3, 6, 9	He would be worshiped by wise men and presented with gifts.	Matthew 2:11

Numbers 24:8 Hosea 11:1	He would be in Egypt for a season.	Matthew 2:15
Jeremiah 31:1	His birthplace would suffer a massacre of infants.	Matthew 2:17–18
Isaiah 11:1	He would be called a Nazarene.	Matthew 2:23
Psalm 69:9; 119:139	He would be zealous for the Father.	John 6:37–40
Psalm 45:7 Isaiah 11:2; 61:1–2	He would be filled with God's Spirit.	Luke 4:18–19
Isaiah 53:4	He would heal many.	Matthew 8:16–17
Isaiah 9:1–2; 42:1–3	He would deal gently with the Gentiles.	Matthew 4:13–16, 12:17–21
Isaiah 6:9–10	He would speak in parables.	Matthew 13:10–15
Psalm 69:8 Isaiah 53:3	He would be rejected by his own.	John 1:11, 7:5
Zechariah 9:9	He would come riding on a young donkey triumphantly into Jerusalem.	Mark 11:1–11
Psalm 8:2	He would be praised by little children.	Matthew 21:16
Psalm 118:22–23	He would be the rejected cornerstone.	Matthew 21:42
Isaiah 53:1	His miracles would not be believed.	John 12:37–38

Psalm 41:9, 55:12–14 Zechariah 11:12–13	His friend would betray him for thirty pieces of silver.	Matthew 26:14–16, 21–25
Isaiah 53:3	He would be a man of sorrows.	Matthew 26:37–38
Zechariah 13:7	He would be forsaken by his disciples.	Matthew 26:31, 56
Isaiah 50:6	He would be scourged and spat upon.	Matthew 26:67, 27:26
Isaiah 53:7	He would remain silent when cruelly treated.	Mark 15:3–5
Jeremiah 18:1–4, 19:1–4 Zechariah 11:12–13	His price would be used to buy a potter's field.	Matthew 27:9–10
Isaiah 53:5	He would suffer on behalf of others.	Romans 5:6–8
Isaiah 53:12	He would be crucified between two thieves.	Matthew 27:38 Mark 15:27–28 Luke 22:37
Psalm 69:21	He would be given vinegar to drink.	Matthew 27:34, 48 John 19:28–30
Psalm 22:16 Zechariah 12:10	He would suffer piercing of his hands and feet.	Mark 15:25 John 19:34, 37; 20:25–27
Psalm 22:18	His garments would be parted and gambled for.	Luke 23:34 John 19:23–24

Psalm 22:7–8	He would be surrounded and ridiculed by his enemies.	Matthew 27:39–44 Mark 15:29–32
Psalm 22:15	He would thirst.	John 19:28
Psalm 31:5	He would commend his spirit to the Father.	Luke 23:46
Exodus 12:46 Number 9:12 Psalm 34:20	His bones would not be broken.	John 19:33–36
Zechariah 12:10	He would be stared at in death.	Matthew 27:36 John 19:37
Isaiah 53:9	He would be buried with the rich.	Matthew 27:57–60
Psalm 16:10, 49:15	His body wouldn't decay; God would redeem him from the grave.	Mark 16:6–7
Psalm 24:7–10	He would ascend.	Mark 16:19 Luke 24:51
Psalm 110:4	He would then become a greater high priest than Aaron.	Hebrews 5:4–6, 10; 7:11–28
Psalm 110:1	He would be seated at God's right hand.	Matthew 22:44 Hebrews 10:12–13
Numbers 24:17 Daniel 2:44–45	He would become a smiting scepter.	Revelation 19:15
Psalm 2:8	He would rule the heathen.	Revelation 2:27

Now let's examine just ten of the prophecies concerning Jesus in more detail.

1. Jesus would come from the line of Abraham.

> Abram fell facedown, and God said to him, "As for me, this is my covenant with you: You will be the father of many nations. No longer will you be called Abram; your name will be Abraham, for I have made you a father of many nations. I will make you very fruitful; I will make nations of you, and kings will come from you. I will establish my everlasting covenant between me and you and your descendants after you." (Genesis 17:3–7)

These scriptures were spoken from God to Abraham some fourteen hundred years before they came true. In the New Testament, Jesus's lineage traces to Abraham:

> *Abraham* was the father of Isaac, Isaac the father of Jacob, Jacob the father of Judah and his brothers, Judah the father of Perez and Zerah, whose mother was Tamar, Perez the father of Hezron, Hezron the father of Ram, Ram the father of Amminadab, Amminadab the father of Nahshon, Nahshon the father of Salmon, Salmon the father of Boaz, whose mother was Rahab, Boaz the father of Obed, whose mother was Ruth, Obed the father of Jesse, and Jesse the father of *King David.* David was the father of *Solomon*, whose mother had been Uriah's wife, Solomon the father of *Rehoboam*, Rehoboam the father of *Abijah*, Abijah the father of *Asa*, Asa the father of *Jehoshaphat*, Jehoshaphat the father of *Jehoram*, Jehoram the father of *Uzziah*, Uzziah

> the father of *Jotham*, Jotham the father of *Ahaz*, Ahaz the father of *Hezekiah*, Hezekiah the father of Manasseh, Manasseh the father of Amon, Amon the father of Josiah, and Josiah the father of Jeconiah and his brothers at the time of the exile to Babylon. After the exile to Babylon: Jeconiah was the father of Shealtiel, Shealtiel the father of Zerubbabel, Zerubbabel the father of Abiud, Abiud the father of Eliakim, Eliakim the father of Azor, Azor the father of Zadok, Zadok the father of Akim, Akim the father of Eliud, Eliud the father of Eleazar, Eleazar the father of Matthan, Matthan the father of Jacob, and Jacob the father of Joseph, the husband of Mary, of whom was born *Jesus*, who is called Christ. (Matthew 1:2–16)

Jesus is the everlasting King, thus fulfilling the covenant God made with Abraham. Further, a number of kings of Israel were in Jesus's genealogy as shown italicized in the text, just as God stated. Amazing!

2. Jesus would come from Bethlehem.

> But you, Bethlehem Ephrathah, though you are small among the clans of Judah, out of you will come for me one who will be ruler over Israel, whose origins are from of old, from ancient time. (Micah 5:2)

This prophecy foretold, over seven hundred years in advance, Jesus would come from the little town of Bethlehem.

> So Joseph also went up from the town of Nazareth in Galilee to Judea, to Bethlehem the town of

> David, because he belonged to the house and line of David. He went there to register with Mary, who was pledged to be married to him and was expecting a child. While they were there, the time came for the baby to be born, and she gave birth to her firstborn, a son. She wrapped him in cloths and place him in a manger, because there was no room for them in the inn. (Luke 2:4–7)

The Roman Empire controlled the Promised Land during the time of Jesus. The emperor, Caesar Augustus, issued a decree for a census to be taken and everyone had to return to their hometown to be counted. This is what precipitated Mary and Joseph traveling to Bethlehem at the time of Jesus's birth. Again, the prophecy was fulfilled exactly as it was foretold hundreds of years in advance.

3. Jesus would be born from a virgin and his name would mean "God with us," Immanuel.

> Therefore the Lord himself will give you a sign: The virgin will be with child and will give birth to a son, and will call him Immanuel. (Isaiah 7:14)

This prophecy from Isaiah is a familiar passage often quoted in Christmas plays and was written hundreds of years before Jesus's birth.

> This is how the birth of Jesus Christ came about: His mother Mary was pledged to be married to Joseph, but before they came together, she was found to be with child through the Holy Spirit. Because Joseph her husband was a righteous man and did not want to expose her to public disgrace he had in mind to divorce her quietly. But after he

> had considered this, an angel of the Lord appeared to him in a dream and said, "Joseph, son of David, do not be afraid to take Mary home as your wife, because what is conceived in her is from the Holy Spirit. She will give birth to a son, and you are to give him the name Jesus, because he will save his people from their sins." All this took place to fulfill what the Lord had said through the prophet: "The virgin will be with child and will give birth to a son, and they will call him Immanuel"—which means, "God with us." When Joseph woke up, he did what the angel of the Lord has commanded him and took Mary home as his wife. But he had no union with her until she gave birth to a son. And he gave him the name Jesus. (Matthew 1:18–25)

Just as prophesied, the Holy Spirit came upon Mary and she became pregnant, though she was not married to Joseph yet and was still a virgin.

4. Jesus would be worshiped by wise men and presented with gifts.

> The kings of Tarshish and of distant shores will bring tribute to him; the kings of Sheba and Seba will present him gifts. (Psalm 71:10)

> Nations will come to your light, and kings to the brightness of your dawn. (Isaiah 60:3)

> Herds of camels will cover your land, young camels of Midian and Ephah. And all from Sheba will come, bearing gold and incense and proclaiming the praise of the Lord. (Isaiah 60:6)

> Surely the islands look to me; in the lead are the ships of Tarshish, bring your sons from afar, with their silver and gold, to the honor of the Lord your God, the Holy One of Israel, for he has endowed you with splendor. (Isaiah 60:9)

The prophecy from Psalms dates to the time of King David, over nine hundred years before the birth of Jesus. The prophecies from Isaiah predate the birth of Jesus by seven hundred years.

> After Jesus was born in Bethlehem in Judea, during the time of King Herod, Magi from the east came to Jerusalem and asked, "Where is the one who has been born king of the Jews? We saw his star in the east and have come to worship him." (Matthew 2:1–2)

> On coming to the house, they saw the child with his mother Mary, and they bowed down and worshiped him. Then they opened their treasures and presented him with gifts of gold and of incense and of myrrh. (Matthew 2:11)

Just as prophesied, wise men came from afar to see the baby Jesus and presented him with gifts.

5. Jesus would be in Egypt for a season.

> When Israel was a child, I loved him, and out of Egypt I called my son. (Hosea 11:1)

This prophecy in Hosea dates to over seven hundred years before the birth of Jesus.

> When they had gone, an angel of the Lord appeared to Joseph in a dream. "Get up," he said, "Take the child and his mother and escape to Egypt. Stay there until I tell you, for Herod is going to search for the child to kill him." So he got up, took the child and his mother during the night and left for Egypt, where he stayed until the death of Herod. And so was fulfilled what the Lord had said through the prophet; "Out of Egypt I called my son." (Matthew 2:13–15)

The Roman King Herod was suspicious and jealous of the baby Jesus and wanted him dead. The angel of the Lord who appeared to Joseph told him to flee from Bethlehem to Egypt for safety. This is exactly what Joseph, Mary, and the baby Jesus did.

6. Jesus's birthplace would suffer a massacre of infants.

> A voice is heard of Ramah, mourning and great weeping, Rachel weeping for her children and refusing to be comforted, because her children are no more. (Jeremiah 31:15)

This prophecy in Jeremiah concerns the massacre of children in Ramah issued by King Herod over six hundred years later.

> When Herod realized that he had been outwitted by the Magi, he was furious, and he gave orders to kill all the boys in Bethlehem and its vicinity who were two years old and under, in accordance with the time he had learned from the Magi. Then what was said through the prophet Jeremiah was fulfilled: "A voice is heard of Ramah, mourning and great weeping, Rachel weeping for her children and

> refusing to be comforted, because her children are no more." (Matthew 2:16–18)

On their way to see Jesus, the Magi first visited with King Herod inquiring about the baby Jesus. King Herod instructed them when they find him, to come back and let him know. King Herod's intent was to kill the baby Jesus. Realizing this, the Magi, after finding and visiting with the baby Jesus, returned to their home country by a different route to avoid tipping off King Herod. When King Herod realized the Magi avoided him, he issued the decree to kill all male babies under the age of two in the Bethlehem area, just as prophecy had forewarned.

7. **Jesus would come riding on a young donkey triumphantly into Jerusalem.**

> Rejoice greatly, O Daughter of Zion! Shout, Daughter of Jerusalem! See, your king comes to you, righteous and having salvation, gentle and riding on a donkey, on a colt, the foal of a donkey. (Zechariah 9:9)

The prophecy in Zechariah was written over five hundred years prior to this actual event.

> They went and found a colt outside in the street, tied at a doorway. As they untied it, some people standing there asked, "What are you doing, untying that colt?" They answered as Jesus had told them to, and the people let them go. When they brought the colt to Jesus and threw their cloaks over it, he sat on it. Many people spread their cloaks on the road, while others spread branches they had cut in the fields. Those who went ahead and those who

> followed shouted, "Hosanna! "Blessed is he who comes in the name of the Lord!" "Blessed is the coming kingdom of our father David!" "Hosanna in the highest!" Jesus entered Jerusalem and went to the temple. (Mark 11:4–10)

This was the first Palm Sunday. Just as prophesied, Jesus came riding into Jerusalem on a donkey while the people put palm tree branches in front of his path to praise and herald him as a king.

8. Jesus's friend would betray him for thirty pieces of silver.

> I told them, "If you think it best, give me my pay; but if not, keep it." So they paid me thirty pieces of silver. And the Lord said to me, "Throw it to the potter—the handsome price at which they priced me! So I took the thirty pieces of silver and threw them into the house of the Lord to the potter. (Zechariah 11:12–13)

Again, this prophecy from Zechariah was written over five hundred years prior to the actual event.

> The one of the Twelve—the one called Judas Iscariot—went to the chief priests and asked, "What are you willing to give me if I hand him over to you?" So they counted out for him thirty silver coins. (Matthew 26:14–15)

Judas Iscariot was one of Jesus's twelve disciples and also the money handler for the group. His love of money overcame his love for Jesus, and he agreed to tip off the chief priests of the Jewish Sanhedrin as to his whereabouts in the middle of the night for thirty pieces of silver. The Pharisees were jealous of Jesus, and by their religious legalism, they failed to see who Jesus really was and plotted to kill him. It was the Pharisees who turned the people against Jesus, even though just a few days before these same people lauded him as king when he entered Jerusalem. After Jesus's arrest, Judas Iscariot realized how big of a mistake he had made and threw the thirty pieces of silver back to the Pharisees. It was too late. The money was used to buy the potter's field outside Jerusalem as a burial place where Judas Iscariot went and committed suicide.

9. Jesus would be crucified between two thieves.

> Therefore I will give him a portion among the great, and he will divide the spoils with the strong, because he poured out his life unto death, and was numbered with the transgressors. For he bore the sin of many, and made intercessions for the transgressors. (Isaiah 53:12)

This passage of scripture, foretelling that Jesus would be "numbered with the transgressors" or law breakers, is dated to around 700 BC.

> They crucified two robbers with him, one on his right and one on his left. (Mark 15:27)

When Jesus was crucified, he was crucified between two sinners, thus "numbering him with the transgressors" and fulfilling prophecy.

10. Jesus would suffer piercing of his hands and feet.

> Dogs have surrounded me; a band of evil men has encircled me, they have pierced my hands and my feet. I can count all my bones; people stare and gloat

> over me. They divide my garments among them and cast lots for my clothing. (Psalm 22:16–18)

The book of Psalms, foretelling of Jesus's hands and feet being pierced and casting lots for his clothing, dates to around 990 BC to the time of King David, who wrote most of the Psalms.

> When the soldiers crucified Jesus, they took his clothes, dividing them into four shares, one for each of them, with the undergarment remaining. This garment was seamless, woven in one piece from top to bottom. "Let's not tear it," they said to one another. "Let's decide by lot who will get it." (John 19:23–24)

Each of the gospels gives an account of the crucifixion of Jesus where the Romans drove spikes into his hands and feet to hold him to the cross, as was prophesied. After his resurrection, Jesus appeared to the disciples, including the "doubting Thomas," where he told him to physically examine his piercings.

> Then he said to Thomas, "Put your finger here; see my hands. Reach out your hand and put it into my side. Stop doubting and believe." Thomas said to him, "My Lord and my God!" (John 20:27–28)

It would be somewhat easy to casually read through these ten fulfilled prophecies without grasping how convincing the proof is that Jesus, and Jesus alone, fulfilled the criteria of being the prophesied Savior the Old Testament spoke about. In doing so, this would also overlook the evidence of the divine influence on the writing of the Bible.

Stop for a moment and consider the statistical odds of each of the ten prophecies coming true in one individual. As an extremely conservative estimate, let's assume the odds of any one of the ten prophecies randomly being fulfilled is one in one hundred. The combined odds for one person fulfilling all ten of the mutually independent prophecies is not ten times one hundred or one in one thousand; it is one in 10^{12}. If you are not familiar with numerical powers, 10^{12} is equivalent to a million times a million, or 1,000 billion. That is larger than the number of people who ever walked on the face of the earth. There can be no doubt Jesus is the prophesied Savior of the Old Testament. However, if you are still not impressed with the divine implications of these prophecies, consider just one prophecy in the Bible concerning Jesus from the book of Daniel written around 540 BC.[3]

> Know and understand this: From the issuing of the decree to restore and rebuild Jerusalem until the Anointed One, the ruler, comes, there will be seven "sevens," and sixty-two "sevens." (Daniel 9:25)

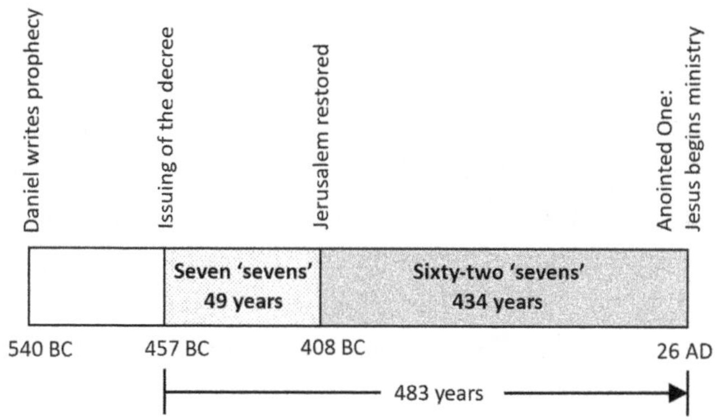

Figure 8.1: Daniel 9:25 accurately predicts Jesus's coming 566 years in advance

Now let's unpack this prophecy to fully appreciate how impressive it is. First, "Issuing of the decree" refers to King Artaxerxes of Persia decree to Ezra and the Israelites in 457 BC. Recall it was King

Cyrus of Persia who defeated the Babylonians and initially freed the Israelites in 536 BC to return to their homeland. But from 536 BC to 457 BC the Israelites struggled with no real government or country and were still under the ruling thumb of Persia. It was not until King Artaxerxes issued his decree in 457 BC that gave Israel the right to self-government and to be recognized as a nation. From this point forward, the Israelites could rebuild their temple and the city of Jerusalem in earnest. "Restore and rebuild Jerusalem" refers to the Israelites rebuilding their city. The "Anointed One" is the Christ. In the Bible "sevens" is a week of years or seven years. "Seven 'sevens'" is seven times seven or forty-nine years. "Sixty-two 'sevens'" is 434 years. Finally, "Seven 'sevens' and sixty-two 'sevens'" is 483 years.

Now we can put it all together. Daniel wrote this prophecy in approximately 540 BC. The issuing of the decree occurred eighty-three years later in 457 BC. Jerusalem was restored and rebuilt forty-nine years later (seven 'sevens') by the year 408 BC. Then, 434 years later (sixty-two "sevens"), or AD 26, Daniel prophesied the Christ would come.

We now know our modern Roman calendar is off four years on the start date since Jesus was born in 4 BC. This is due to an error of a sixth century AD Roman monk-mathematician-astronomer named Dionysius Exiguus.[3] He set the calendar to center around Jesus's birth, but incorrectly placed Jesus's birth to the year of King Herod's death. Jesus, however, was born at least four years prior. But once it was established, it has never been corrected.

From the Bible we learn Jesus was thirty years old when he started his ministry. Go forward thirty years from 4 BC and we arrive at AD 26. AD 26 is exactly as Daniel had predicted it back in 540 BC! How do you explain or account for this prophecy other than there was a divine influence on the writer? Coincidence?

Perhaps you are thinking at this point that the prophecies did not predate the actual occurrence of the event or Jesus. The prophecies are too good and too accurate to be real. Perhaps the Old Testament prophecies were written *after* the event actually took place. Hmm?

Let's now consider the evidence obtained from the Dead Sea Scrolls. Although there have been literally thousands of biblical manuscripts discovered by archeologists, the greatest find came in 1947.[4] That is when a Bedouin shepherd boy was searching for a lost stray from his sheep and goat flock among the rocky crags roughly one mile from the northwest shore of the Dead Sea. He spotted a cave jutting out from the rocks and threw a rock into it, hoping he would perhaps hear from his stray. Instead he heard the sound of a clay jar breaking. He climbed inside the cave to find hundreds of clay jars containing old manuscripts. His find in the Qumran caves became known as the Dead Sea Scrolls. In all over two hundred clay pots containing 981 different texts were discovered in eleven caves in the area. The scrolls were dated from the third century BC to the first century AD. Interestingly, the Dead Sea is one of the driest places on earth, and this helped preserve the manuscripts for such a lengthy period of time.[5] Another coincidence?

Figure 8.2: Qumran caves where Dead Sea Scrolls were found

The scrolls of the scriptures are over a thousand years older than any of the previous manuscripts found. This is important for two reasons. First and foremost, the date of the scrolls containing the Old

Testament prophecies, including those concerning Jesus, predated Jesus. This is important because for the first time, there is actual written proof the prophecies concerning Jesus were made before he appeared on earth. This dispels any notion the Old Testament prophecies and scripture were written after the fact to create the appearance of fulfilled prophecies. Second, the scriptures, separated by over a thousand years, agreed to within 95 percent accuracy on a word for word basis.[6] The differences are mostly slips of the pen or spelling. This is proof the scrolls were copied very carefully through the years.

Figure 8.3: Dead Sea Scroll

So in summary, there are over one thousand prophecies in the Bible concerning people, cities, and nations. There are over three hundred prophecies on Jesus alone. We have hard, factual evidence the prophecies predated the actual historical event by hundreds of years, and the prophecies were fulfilled exactly as predicted. There is no other explanation for this other than divine influence. So collectively we now have evidence the Christian faith and the Bible are grounded on factual evidence supporting the scientific, historical, and geographical trustworthiness of the Bible—and now strong evidence of divine influence! Coincidence?

Chapter 9

New Testament-Era Evidence

4 BC–AD 60

During my sophomore year of undergraduate studies, the issue of evolution versus creationism became the hot topic in the student newspaper. The battle lines were drawn as students from both sides of the debate would weigh in daily with their thoughts and comments on why or why not God exists. During this time an unofficial student leader of the atheist side emerged. He was the most outspoken and hard-hitting of the entire evolutionary voices. Imagine my surprise when I learned he lived on my dorm floor. I did not know him personally at the time but learned who he was, and we would exchange the obligatory hi and "how's it going" in passing.

Something internally urged me to take action. Even though I was swamped with the rigor of engineering classes and working in the school cafeteria, I needed to do something. But what? Then it occurred to me that during my freshman year while moving in, I was befriended by an elderly guy from the local city where the college was located. He graciously helped carry my belongings from the parking lot up the several flights of stairs to my dorm room. In thanking and talking with him afterward, it became known he was a Christian and also a Korean War veteran. He had given me his number and said if he could ever be of help, give him a call. Good thing I kept his number because the vocal student leader of the atheists was an ROTC or Reserve Officer Training Cadet. He was preparing for a life in the military, and with the elderly guy being a veteran, perhaps his presence could possibly interest him in joining a weekly Bible study.

So I contacted the elderly guy from the city and shared my thoughts concerning a dorm room Bible study and inviting an outspoken atheist advocate from my floor. He was on board immediately. Next up was to invite the vocal atheist student leader. After running into him in the dorm hallway, I simply explained to him what I was up to and that we would enjoy his participation. He simply responded yes. With the addition of my roommate and a couple others, thus began a weekly Bible study in our dorm room. As you can imagine, in the small, tightly crammed dorm room, with beds lofted above the underlying study desks, it was almost shoulder to shoulder for a half-dozen guys to huddle around in chairs for a study.

As you might also imagine, the group dynamics were very interesting. In one corner was the elderly, calm, and collected statesman who had been in the trenches from a military perspective and emerged as a steadfast Christian. In the other corner was the young, fiery charismatic student who aspired to be a military leader, but also a dyed-in-the-wool atheist. The mutual respect toward each other was apparent from the very first discussion. We read and studied from the book of John, one of the gospels in the New Testament.

During our time of study, the student leader was very cordial and respectful to all those in the study. However, his daily rants in the comment section of the paper continued as before. But over time, an interesting thing emerged. His attacks became less frequent and his tone softer. Then one day, they ceased entirely. He stopped writing comments into the school paper questioning the existence of God, and with him silenced, a ceasefire happened in the school paper as other atheist contributors stopped their assaults as well.

Having been there firsthand to see how it all rolled out, it is amazing how God can orchestrate events. To this day, I do not know what happened to him and whether he put down his biased guard long enough to critically examine the evidence concerning Jesus and form an unbiased opinion based on fact, rather than emotions. If so, it would not surprise me if he is off in a dorm room somewhere trying to lead others to Christ himself.

In the previous chapters, we stepped through time in the Old Testament and looked at the evidence along the way in support of Christianity. Now, like my college dorm room Bible study, we will focus our attention on the period from the birth of Jesus through the initial birth and growth of Christianity, or essentially the first half of the first century AD.

In brief summary, the New Testament tells us the Savior, Jesus, has come, whereas the Old Testament points out the need for a savior. The first four books of the New Testament, the gospels Matthew, Mark, Luke, and John, give details concerning the life, death, and resurrection of Jesus. The rest of the New Testament details the growth of the Christian Church and how followers of Jesus, Christians, should conduct their lives until Jesus returns to Earth again.

In this chapter we will only touch on some of the archeological and historical evidence backing up the New Testament events, locations, cities, people and Jesus. The next two chapters will be devoted to Jesus alone. There is a large amount of evidence external to the Bible validating the life, death, and resurrection of Jesus. In fact, if we were to put the Bible aside for a moment, we would know all the major facets of Jesus life from external sources alone, as we will see in the pages ahead.

We will not dwell extensively on any one event or period but just look at a smattering of the archeological evidence supporting the New Testament of the Bible. Again, of the thousands of ancient artifacts, cities, structures, and inscriptions that have been unearthed, not one contradicts the Bible.

So let's pick up the trail of the archeological evidence as we continue to walk through the Bible chronologically.

4 BC – Birth of Jesus

The birth of Jesus, and many details surrounding his birth, were prophesied hundreds of years before the event occurred as we looked at in the previous chapter. But in this chapter, we will look only at archeological evidence. The Roman Empire controlled the area in which Jesus was born and lived throughout his life on earth. The Roman Emperor Caesar Augustus issued a decree requiring a census to be taken and everyone had to go to their ancestral hometown to register and pay taxes. This is what caused Jesus's parents, Mary and Joseph, to travel to Bethlehem.

> In those days Caesar Augustus issued a decree that a census should be taken of the entire Roman world. (This was the first census that took place while Quirinius was governor of Syria.) And everyone went to his own town to register. So Joseph also went up from the town of Nazareth in Galilee to Judea, to Bethlehem the town of David, because he belonged to the house and line of David. He went there to register with Mary, who was pledged to be married to him and was expecting a child. While they were there, the time came for the baby to be born, and she gave birth to her firstborn, a son. She wrapped him in cloths and place him in a manger, because there was no room for them in the inn. (Luke 2:1–7)

> After Jesus was born in Bethlehem in Judea. (Matthew 2:1)

Archeology has uncovered many artifacts identifying the Roman emperor, Caesar Augustus, who issued the decree, causing Joseph and Mary to travel to Bethlehem. These artifacts include sculptures and coins with his image. One such artifact, a bronze bust[1] depicting him riding on a horse, is housed in the National Archeological Museum in Athens.

When Mary and Joseph arrived in Bethlehem, there was no room at the inn, so Mary placed the baby Jesus in a manger that was normally used to feed animals. From this, it has been assumed Jesus was born in a stable. Archeology has shown the use of caves as livestock stables was a common practice in the area at this time. On the outskirts of ancient Bethlehem is a building named the Church of the Nativity standing over a cave claimed to be the actual birthplace of Jesus.[2] It has been there since AD 326, and records show for at least two hundred years before the church was built, Christians honored this cave as the birthplace of Jesus.

Figure 9.1: Modern-day Bethlehem

Before we leave the birth of Jesus, it's worth a short discussion on the terms BC and AD as applied to calendar year. Recall BC stands for "before Christ" and AD stands for "anno Domini," which is shortened for "Anno Domini Nostri Iesu Christi," which is ancient Latin for "in the year of our Lord Jesus Christ." Jesus's birth literally split history in two: BC to the time before his birth and AD to the time after his birth. As previously discussed, a sixth-century AD

Roman monk incorrectly placed Jesus's birth, and the four-year error has never been corrected.[3]

After Jesus's birth, Mary and Joseph fled to Egypt to escape the murderous wrath of King Herod who sought to kill Jesus after the wise men who visited the baby Jesus told the king of his birth. After King Herod's death, the Bible tells us Mary and Joseph returned to the town of Nazareth with Jesus to live:

> And he went and lived in a town called Nazareth.
> So was fulfilled what was said through the prophets:
> "He will be called a Nazarene." (Matthew 2:23)

Like Bethlehem, the town of Nazareth is still a bustling city in the southern hills of Galilee that you can go to today. The people and places surrounding the birth of Jesus as described in the Bible are real, historical people and places.

Figure 9.2: Modern-day Nazareth

Now fast-forward the clock about thirty years to the approximate three-year period during Jesus's ministry following his baptism by John the Baptist.

AD 26—Jesus's Ministry

The first recorded miracle of Jesus involves turning water into wine at a wedding in Cana:

> On the third day a wedding took place at Cana in Galilee. Jesus' mother was there, and Jesus and his disciples had also been invited to the wedding. (John 2:1–2)

The account is given in the Bible in the book of John. Archeologists have located the ruins of the village of Cana about nine miles north of Nazareth.

Figure 9.3: Modern-day Cana in Galilee

Peter was one of Jesus's disciples, and the Bible gives an account of Jesus healing Peter's mother-in-law:

> When Jesus came into Peter's house, he saw Peter's mother-in-law lying in bed with a fever. He touched

> her hand and the fever left her, and she got up and began to wait on him. (Matthew 8:14)

In 1968 archeologists discovered the church building they were studying was built over a house dated to the time of Jesus.[4] There are engravings on the walls of the house that indicate the early Christians believed the house was that of the disciple Peter.

Figure 9.4: Remains of house believed to be that of disciple Peter

Jesus often taught in the synagogues as he traveled around the countryside. One such town mentioned throughout the gospels is Capernaum:

> He said this while teaching in the synagogue in Capernaum. (John 6:59)

Capernaum served as Jesus's base during his ministry in the Galilee area. He taught and healed in the synagogue. The synagogue from Jesus's time has been unearthed in Capernaum buried underneath another synagogue built on top of it over three hundred years later.[5]

Figure 9.5: Ruins of Capernaum synagogue where Jesus taught

The Bible records Jesus had great compassion and healed and drove out demons from people. One such event happened on the east side of the Sea of Galilee:

> When he arrived at the other side in the region of the Gadarenes, two demon-possessed men coming from the tombs met him. Some distance from them a large herd of pigs was feeding. The demons begged Jesus, "If you drive us out, send us into the herd of pigs." He said to them, "Go!" So they came out and went into the pigs, and the whole herd rushed down the steep bank into the lake and died in the water. (Matthew 8:28, 30–32)

The steep bank on the edge of the Sea of Galilee where this occurred remained a mystery until 1970. In that year archeologist Vasilios Tzaferis discovered an ancient Christian church, building, monastery, and chapels at the foot of a steep slope on the east side of the Sea of Galilee. This led him to conclude the buildings were probably built there by ancient Christians to preserve the spot where Jesus drove out the demons.[6]

A somewhat familiar Bible passage to most Christians is an encounter between Jesus and a less-than-virtuous Samaritan woman at Jacob's well:

> Now he had to go through Samaria. So he came to a town in Samaria called Sychar, near the plot of ground Jacob had given to his son Joseph. Jacob's well was there, and Jesus, tired as he was from the journey, sat down by the well. (John 4:4–6)

The gospel of John goes on to describe an encounter at the well between Jesus and the Samaritan woman. This well still exists today and is located beside an ancient north-south road near Mount Gerizim, east of Nablus.[7]

Figure 9.6: 1894 photo of Jacob's well

The Bible records Jesus healing many people, such as the man at the pool at Bethesda:

> Now there is in Jerusalem near the Sheep Gate a pool, which in Aramaic is called Bethesda and which is surrounded by five covered colonnades. (John 5:2)

At this location Jesus healed a paralyzed man. The ruins of the pool have been located, and portions of the five colonnades still exists.[8]

Figure 9.7: Pool at Bethesda

Again and again, places and structures mentioned in the Bible have been authenticated by archeology, such as the city of Caesarea Philippi:

> Jesus and his disciples went on to the village around Caesarea Philippi. (Mark 8:27)

It was at Caesarea Philippi where Peter was the first of the disciples to acknowledge and state Jesus was the prophesied Christ or Savior of the world. In response, Jesus declared this was revealed to Peter by God.

Figure 9.8: Caesarea Philippi

Another somewhat-famous passage of scripture of Jesus healing occurred at the pool of Siloam:

> Having said this, he spit on the ground, made some mud with the saliva, and put it on the man's eyes. "Go," he told him, "wash in the Pool of Siloam" (meaning Sent). So the man went and washed, and came home seeing. (John 9:6–7)

As described, at the Pool of Siloam Jesus healed a blind man. The pool was discovered in 2004, along with coins found in the area dating to Jesus's era, indicating the pool was in use during Jesus's time.[9]

Figure 9.9: Pool of Siloam in Jerusalem

A group of ten cities, known as the Decapolis, is mentioned a couple of times in the New Testament:

> Large crowds from Galilee, the Decapolis, Jerusalem, Judea and the region across the Jordan followed him. (Matthew 4:25)

The Decapolis was a group of ten cities: Damascus, Abila, Scythopolis, Hippos, Raphana, Gadara, Pella, Dion, Philadelphia, and Gerasa. They are mentioned in both Matthew and Mark as regions where Jesus's message was spread. Archeologists have located and excavated nine of the cities, and only Dion remains in question.[10]

Figure 9.10: Beth Shen (Scythopolis), one of the ten cities of the Decapolis

After years of scrutiny and examination by critics and skeptics alike, Luke, the author of the gospel Luke and the book of Acts, has come to be known as a very detailed, accurate, and highly trustworthy historian. In his book he gives the following account:

> In the fifteenth year of the reign of Tiberius Caesar—when Pontius Pilate was governor of Judea, Herod tetrarch of Galilee, his brother Philip tetrarch of Iturea and Traconitis, and Lysanias tetrarch of Abilene—during the high priesthood of Annas and Caiaphas, the word of God came to John son of Zechariah in the desert. (Luke 3:1–2)

Many skeptics had scoffed at Luke because he wrote "Lysanias tetrarch of Abilene" and the only known Lysanias died in 36 BC. Then an inscription was found, dating to AD 14–29, in Abila stating "Nymphias, freedman of Lysanias the tetrarch," providing strong evidence Luke was indeed correct once again.[11]

Yet another example of Luke originally being scoffed at and then later proven to be an accurate historian involved the use of the term politarchs.

> The city officials. (Acts 17:6)

Politarchs is translated as "city official" and was not used by others in this timeframe, or so it was thought. Then a stone artifact was found from Luke's era where another historian used the term *politarchs*, thus dispelling this notion. This and numerous other archeological finds have proven Luke to be an accurate historian.

AD 30—Crucifixion of Jesus

Now let's move forward to the time of Jesus's crucifixion. We will cover more details of the crucifixion and resurrection in later chapters, but for now let's examine some of the archeological evidence supporting this event.

The Romans began practicing crucifixion in the third century BC. Artifacts of crucifixion in Rome, such as a heel bone found with a spike embedded into it, gives credibility death by crucifixion as described in the Bible was practiced by Rome during Jesus's timeframe.

After Jesus's arrest, he was first brought to the Jewish religious ruling body, the Sanhedrin, who were led by the high priest Caiaphas:

> Then the detachment of soldiers with its commander and the Jewish officials arrested Jesus. They bound him and brought him first to Annas, who was the father-in-law of Caiaphas, the high priest that year. (John 18:12–13)

The stone box, or ossuary, containing the bones of Caiaphas may have been found in 1990. In a first-century AD burial cave south of Jerusalem, an ossuary was accidently found that had the name "Caiaphas" engraved on it that contained the bones of a dead man.[12] The ossuary is housed as part of the collection in the Israel Museum in Jerusalem.

Pontius Pilate was the weak-willed Roman governor over Jerusalem who gave in to the will of the Jewish religious leaders, who had stirred up the crowd that led to the crucifixion of Jesus:

> In the fifteenth year of the reign of Tiberius Caesar—when Pontius Pilate was governor of Judea. (Luke 3:1)

> Indeed Herod and Pontius Pilate met together with the Gentiles and the people of Israel in this city to conspire against your holy servant, Jesus, who you anointed. (Acts 4:27)

For many years, Bible naysayers would point to Pontius Pilate as named in Luke 3:1, Acts 4:27, and 1 Timothy 6:13 and point out no artifacts have been found external to the Bible validating his existence. Then in 1961 in Caesarea a stone was found in the ruins of Caesarea Maritima with Pontius Pilate's name on it identifying him.[13] The stone writing commemorates Pontius Pilate's dedication of a temple to Emperor Tiberius. Once more, the Bible was proven accurate in its description of people and places.

Figure 9.11: Stone found in Caesarea in 1961 with Pontius Pilate's name on it

After Jesus was sentenced to death, he was forced to carry his wooden cross to the place of the crucifixion, Golgotha:

> So the soldiers took charge of Jesus. Carrying his own cross, he went out to the place of the Skull (which in Aramaic is called Golgotha). Here they crucified him, and with him two others—one on each side and Jesus in the middle. (John 19:16–18)

Figure 9.12: Golgotha

The spot where Jesus was crucified, called Golgotha, is a real location and can be visited today in the city of Jerusalem.

The Bible records at the moment Jesus died on the cross, the curtain in the holy of holies tore in two:

> With a loud cry, Jesus breathed his last. The curtain of the temple was torn in two from top to bottom. And when the centurion, who stood there in front of Jesus, heard his cry and saw how he died, he said, "Surely this man was the Son of God!" (Mark 15:37–39)

The curtain veiled the holy of holies within the temple in Jerusalem. The tearing of the curtain at Jesus's death signifies all may enter into the presence of God with Jesus as the mediator. Prior to Jesus, only the High Priest could enter the holy of holies. The foundation of the walls of the holy of holies was found underneath the Muslim Dome of the Rock that was built over it centuries later after the temple was destroyed by Romans in AD 70.[14]

Figure 9.13: Trenches cut in rock beneath Dome of the Rock match Biblical dimensions for holy of holies

After Jesus's death, Joseph of Arimathea, a member of the Jewish Sanhedrin, prepared Jesus's body for burial and placed him in a new stone tomb:

> Now there was a man named Joseph, a member of the Council, a good and upright man, who had not consented to their decision and action. He came

> from the Judean town of Arimathea and he was waiting for the kingdom of God. Going to Pilate, he asked for Jesus' body. Then he took it down, wrapped it in linen cloth and placed it in a tomb cut in the rock, one in which no one had yet been laid. (Luke 23:50–53)

Most archeologists believe that the Church of the Holy Sepulcher, built around AD 340, is built over the site of Jesus's burial tomb.[15] It is the site of an old rock quarry dating to the end of the Old Testament, and tombs have been cut into the quarry wall during the first century AD.

Figure 9.14: Church of the Holy Sepulcher

The Bible records a large round stone was rolled in front of Jesus's burial tomb:

> They found the stone rolled away from the tomb, but when they entered, they did not find the body of the Lord Jesus. (Luke 24:2–3)

Examples of the type of tomb Jesus's body was placed in still exist in modern Israel. The tombs were cut in the sides of hills and then a large round stone was rolled in place to block the entrance. After the body decayed, the bones were placed into an ossuary and kept in the central space inside the tomb, where other deceased remains could be kept as well.

Figure 9.15: Ancient burial tomb in Jerusalem

Two very intriguing artifacts discovered concerning the crucifixion of Jesus are the shroud of Turin and the sudarium of Oviedo.[16] [17] Either artifact may have been the actual covering placed over Jesus's body following his death. The shroud covered the entire body, whereas the sudarium was put over the head. The blood type on both artifacts match, AB positive, as do the bloodstain patterns. The shroud of Turin is the single most studied artifact in human history, yet both it and the sudarium remain in a cloud of controversy regarding whether they are the actual garments placed on Jesus's body. The shroud is currently kept in the Cathedral of Saint John the Baptist in Turin, Italy, and the sudarium is kept in a cathedral in northern Spain.

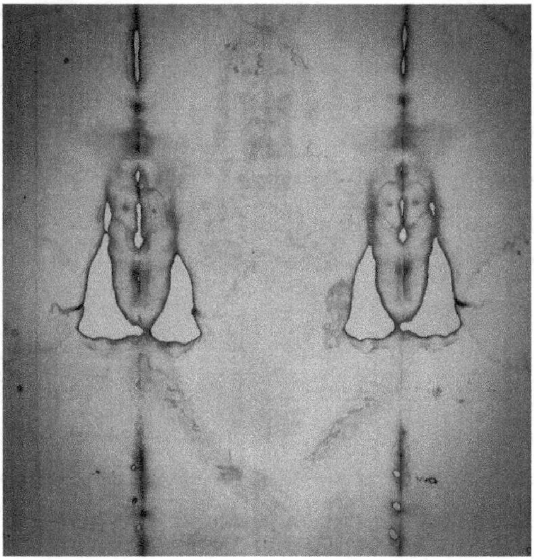

Figure 9.16: Shroud of Turin

One account of the burial clothes in the Bible is given in the book of John:

> Then Simon Peter, who was behind him, arrived and went into the tomb. He saw the strips of linen lying there, as well as the burial cloth that had been around Jesus' head. (John 20:6–7)

AD 30–64—Initial Growth of the Christian Church

With the death, resurrection, and ascension of Jesus, the Bible records the explosive growth of the Christian faith and church primarily throughout the book of Acts. The two main evangelists were Peter and Paul. Peter was one of the disciples of Jesus and preached primarily to the Jews. Paul was a Pharisee, a member of the ruling Jewish Sanhedrin, which invoked the crowd to have Jesus crucified. Paul persecuted Christians by putting them to death. He was on his way to Damascus for this very purpose when the Bible records he had an encounter with the resurrected Jesus. There he met the risen Christ and became an ardent follower of Jesus. His Hebrew name was Saul, but since he evangelized primarily to the gentiles (non-Jews), he went by his Latin name, Paul:

> He went to the high priest and asked him for letters to the synagogues in Damascus, so that if he found any there who belonged to the Way, whether men or women, he might take them as prisoners to Jerusalem. As he neared Damascus on his journey, suddenly a light from heaven flashed around him. …The Lord told him, "Go to the house of Judas on Straight Street and ask for a man from Tarsus named Saul, for he is praying. (Acts 9:2–3, 11)

Damascus is the city where Paul was converted from seeking out Christians (followers of the Way) to put to death, into becoming a follower of Jesus himself. Damascus still exists today in Syria. Excavation of parts of the city has revealed Roman gates and arches and even "Straight Street," as mentioned by name in the Bible, still exists today.

Paul traveled around extensively spreading the good news concerning Jesus. One such town was Caesarea:

> At Caesarea there was a man named Cornelius, a centurion in what was known as the Italian Regiment. (Acts 10:1)

Caesarea was an important city in Jesus's day and the site of several significant biblical events. Most notably it was the town where Paul first had gentiles accept the Christian faith. It was also one of the places he was imprisoned. Excavations in the city have unearthed temples, aqueducts, streets, a theater, and the marketplace.[18]

Figure 9.17: Theater from ancient Caesarea

Another town that Paul preached the gospel message in was Antioch:

> News of this reached the ears of the church at Jerusalem, and they sent Barnabas to Antioch. (Acts 11:22)

Paul and Barnabas evangelized to the diverse people of Antioch, and these people in turn played an important role spreading Christianity throughout the entire Mediterranean region. Today the ancient city of Antioch has been built over by the Turkish city of Antakya.[19] Archeology of the ancient Antioch sitting on the ancient Roman highway revealed it had a diverse population. Antioch was second only to Jerusalem in number of followers of Jesus.

Figure 9.18: Ruins at ancient Antioch

Paul met and preached the gospel messages to many people throughout many locations. One such person was Sergius Paulus:

> There they met a Jewish sorcerer and false prophet named Bar-Jesus, who was an attendant of the proconsul, Sergius Paulus. The proconsul, an intelligent man, sent for Barnabas and Saul because he wanted to hear the word of God. (Acts 13:6–7)

Inscriptions in stone naming Sergius Paulus were discovered in 1877 and 1912, confirming the person encountered by Paul on his missionary journeys.[20]

Another town Paul preached in was Philippi:

> From there we traveled to Philippi, a Roman Colony and the leading city of that district of Macedonia. (Acts 16:12)

Paul preached his first sermon in what is now Europe in the city of Philippi where a woman named Lydia converted to Christianity. He also wrote a letter to the Philippians that became a book of the Bible. The ancient city of Philippi has been excavated revealing carved shrines.

Figure 9.19: Theater in Philippi

Still another town Paul preached in was Ephesus:

> They arrived at Ephesus, where Paul left Priscilla and Aquila. He himself went into the synagogue and reasoned with the Jews. (Acts 18:19)

Ephesus was a large city and is where Paul stayed the longest during his missionary journeys to spread the gospel message to the gentiles. The letter to the Ephesians that became a book of the Bible was written by Paul. Archeologists have recovered much of the ancient city of Ephesus from Paul's day, including the temple of Artemis and the theater where Paul's friends were dragged.

Figure 9.20: Theater in Ephesus

Yet another town Paul preached in was Thessalonica:

> When they had passed through Amphipolis and Apollonia, they came to Thessalonica, where there was a Jewish synagogue. (Acts 17:1)

Paul visited Thessalonica on several occasions, preaching in the synagogue, and was able to start a church there. Two books of the Bible are letters from Paul to the church in Thessalonica. Thessalonica has been excavated and lies along the ancient Roman highway.

Figure 9.21: Theater in Thessalonica

News of Paul spread throughout the Mediterranean, and the people of Athens were anxious to hear him speak:

> Then they took him and brought him to a meeting of the Areopagus, where they said to him, "May we know what this new teaching is that you are presenting?" (Acts 17:19)

The Areopagus was in Athens and was a place of public intellectual discussion. Paul was taken there to present to the Athenians the gospel of Jesus. The Areopagus is on a hill in the center of Athens and has been known by this name since early Christian days. There are two terraces on the hillside, with the upper terrace having cut rock seating for many people.

Figure 9.22: Areopagus hill overlooking Athens

Paul frequently sent greetings in his writings to specific people. In the book of Romans, Paul sent his greetings to Erastus, the city of Corinth's director of public works:

> Erastus, who is the city's director of public works, and our brother Quartus send you their greetings. (Romans 15:24)

In 1929 archeologists found a paving stone in Corinth with Erastus's name stating he was a public official in Corinth.[21]

Many different coins mentioned in the New Testament during Jesus's timeframe have been recovered by archeologists and collectors. These include the denarius with the image of the Roman Emperor Tiberius, as described in Luke 3:1, who ruled from AD 14 to 37 during Jesus's ministry.[22]

These are just a handful of the New Testament archeological finds. There are many more places, such as the Jordan River, the Sea of Galilee, the tomb of Lazarus, and the Upper Room where Jesus ate his last supper, supporting the Bible's account of people places and events. In this regard, Jerusalem has been a real treasure chest with a multitude of buildings and artifacts demonstrating the Bible is an accurate historical document.

Figure 9.23: Jerusalem

Finally, in the last book of the Bible, Revelation, the writer John starts off with messages to seven churches. All seven cities of these churches mentioned in Revelation 1:11 have been found and excavated: Ephesus, Smyrna, Pergamum, Thyatira, Sardis, Philadelphia, and Laodicea. Also from the book of Revelation, John describes the battle of Armageddon, the final battle on earth. The word *Armageddon* comes from the word *Har* that means mountain and the word Megiddo.[23] The valley of Megiddo is a real place in Northern Israel today.

Figure 9.24: Armageddon where the Bible states the final battle will take place

Summary

The archeological evidence support for the Bible and Christian faith from the time period when Jesus was on the earth to the spread of the church in the first century AD, as covered in the New Testament, is extensive. The examples given are just a brief snippet of the thousands of artifacts archeologists have discovered, proving again and again the historical and geographical accuracy of the Bible. The Bible truly is unlike any other book in the world. Again, consider the fact that not one artifact discovered has contradicted the Bible, the Christian faith, or the life of Jesus. Not one. Coincidence?

Chapter 10

Did the Resurrection Really Happen?

AD 30

My first introduction to computers came in college and involved mainframe computers. Beyond handheld calculators, and the emerging Commodore 64 and IBM XT desktop computers, mainframe computers were it. At this time, computer programs were submitted to the mainframe computer in the form of three- by six-inch cards with rectangular holes punched out of them at appropriate locations the computer could read. Each line of computer programming code required one card. So if you had a computer program several hundred lines long, it would require several hundred punched cards stacked together to feed into the computer.

If you have ever written computer programs, then you realize each line of code must be exactly written and in the exact order for the program to work as intended. With the punch cards, there was no simple correction by hitting the backspace key and entering a new value. Any errors in the punch card required punching a new card with the proper rectangular holes punched out. All lines of code had to be visually examined between the original written source code and what was punched into the card. Further, the cards had to be in the exact order. One misplaced card and the program would not run, and a dropped box of cards spelled disaster. Many hours would be spent writing a computer program, punching the cards, putting the cards in order, and then submitting them to the mainframe computer to run. If there was even the slightest error in writing the program, in punching the cards, or putting them in order, the entire program would not work. Everything had to be perfect.

Such is the case with the resurrection. The resurrection of Jesus is the final seal confirming Jesus is the Christ, the anointed Savior of the world. As the Bible proclaims, Jesus is the Son of God, he is fully God and fully man. He lived a sinless life, died for our sins, and rose from the dead. Just as he overcame death, we too can overcome death by placing our trust and faith in him as the Bible states. However, if the resurrection could be disproved, then Christianity itself could be disproved. Like the mainframe computers running on punch cards, one error and everything becomes a house of cards collapsing on itself. So the question is, did Jesus really come back to life after being crucified on the cross? We will look at a dozen or so aspects to this question and then consider the entire body of evidence.

Point 1: The resurrection was a fabricated story.

First let's consider what the gospel writers had to gain by writing their accounts if it was a fabricated story. What they could gain was perhaps some notoriety as a writer with this story. However, what they had to lose for fabricating such a story was their very lives! Followers of Christ were put to death, not glorified on the *New York Times* bestsellers list. After the crucifixion of Jesus, the disciples fled for their lives. But once they saw the resurrected Jesus, they became bold in their actions, including risking death to share the story.

If you think about it, no one was in a better position to know whether Jesus's resurrection was true than his disciples. They spent the previous three years traveling with him, listening to him, watching him, and seeing him perform miracles. So too with the resurrection. Jesus showed himself personally to the disciples after his resurrection so they could see firsthand he had indeed overcome death.

The disciples would know the whole truth concerning Jesus. They were with Jesus before and after the crucifixion and resurrection. They knew the truth. Prior to Jesus's death and resurrection, the disciples were not bold. When Jesus was captured and brought to trial, they mostly fled in fear of their own lives. But following the resurrection and Jesus appearing physically to them, they became strong in their faith and openly risked their lives by spreading Christianity. This gives a high degree of credibility to their story.

In addition, Jesus fulfilled more than fifty prophecies by his death and resurrection alone. These prophecies were made hundreds of years before Jesus even lived. We now have manuscripts from the Dead Seas Scrolls of the Old Testament containing these prophecies, and they predate Jesus by hundreds of years, so we now have solid evidence these prophecies are authentic. These prophecies give further credibility to the resurrection and dispel the notion the resurrection was a fabricated story.

Point 2: Jesus did not die on the cross.

This is the so-called swoon theory claiming Jesus underwent all the physical items described in the Bible, but did not die, recovered while in the tomb, and then escaped.

The first counter to this thought is the Roman soldiers themselves would have been subjected to death if they failed to kill Jesus on the cross. If their own lives were at stake for failure, it is reasonable to assume they would have been certain of his death when they allowed for his removal from the cross.

The actual mechanism of death during crucifixion is the person is no longer able to breathe properly, both bringing in fresh air and expelling spent air from the lungs, causing them to die from asphyxiation. It is akin to drowning. During this process, the person being crucified can use their legs, albeit painfully, since their legs are nailed as well, to straighten up their body and expel the air from their lungs. To accelerate the death process, the Roman soldiers would break people's legs while they were on the cross so they could no longer use their legs to aid their breathing. Consequently death would come much quicker. In the case of Jesus, though, the Roman soldiers did not break Jesus's legs to accelerate death. After the severe floggings and beatings he had already endured, he was dead after six hours of hanging on the cross. Again, the Roman soldiers who risked the same death penalty if they failed would have been certain of Jesus's death and the pointlessness of breaking his legs. Jesus was, however, pierced through his side while on the cross by the soldiers to ensure his death. At this time blood flowed out of Jesus mixed with water, which medically indicates death had occurred.

In addition to the Roman soldiers, there were numerous eyewitnesses who saw Jesus nailed to the cross and then die. If the swoon theory was true, all these eyewitnesses would have been in error.

For the swoon theory to be correct, theorizing Jesus indeed did not die, he would have had to survive the floggings and beatings, being nailed to a wooden cross, and experience the torture of crucifixion for six hours where air does not enter and exit freely from the lungs as well as a stab wound through his side where fluid gushed from his body. After all of this he would have been removed from the cross while not showing any signs of life, including breathing. He would have been placed in a tomb, where under his own power made a recovery sufficient for him to roll away a massive stone blocking the tomb entrance, sneak past four guards, and then make a full recovery. This account seems highly implausible.

Point 3: Everyone went to the wrong tomb.

Although this is a counter theory to Jesus's resurrection, it seems highly unlikely. How could everyone, including the guards, get this wrong? If this happened, Jesus's dead body could have been produced by the guards to immediately disprove Jesus was alive.

Point 4: Jesus's tomb didn't become a shrine.

It was first-century custom to set up a shrine at the site of a holy man's bones. There were at least fifty such sites in Jesus's time.[1] Since there was never a shrine at Jesus's tomb, this would suggest his bones were not contained in a tomb in the area. No shrine, no bones, no death.

Point 5: Jesus's body was stolen.

Matthew's gospel states the Jewish priests and leaders spread this lie:

> While the women were on their way, some of the guards went into the city and reported to the chief priests everything that had happened. When the chief priests met with the elders and devised a plan, they gave the soldiers a large sum of money, telling them, "You are to say, 'His disciples came during the night and stole him away while we were asleep.' If this report gets to the governor, we will satisfy him and keep you out of trouble." So the soldiers took the money and did as they were instructed. And this story has been widely circulated among the Jews to this very day. (Matthew 28:11–15)

If Jesus's body was stolen by the disciples while the guards were asleep, how could the guards know it was the disciples? To know it was the disciples implies they saw them. And if they saw them, why did they not stop them? The guards risked death themselves if they fell asleep while on watch. Matthew's account explains how this account surfaced by the guards being bribed by the Jewish chief priests and elders when they originally reported to the Jewish leader the true account. In addition, Jesus's dead body was never produced.

Point 6: Eyewitnesses were unreliable.

As seen in the previous sections, the Bible, has been proven to be historically accurate. The resurrection is just another historical account the Bible accurately describes. Consider during the time when the gospels were being written, a woman's testimony was not allowed in court. Their testimony had no legal credibility. All four gospels state women were the first eyewitnesses to Jesus's resurrection. If the gospel writers were fabricating a story, they certainly would not have stated women were the first eyewitnesses. So in a backhanded sort of way, the fact the gospel writers state women were the first eyewitnesses actually gives credibility to the fact they were giving accurate accounts of what took place.

Point 7: Many eyewitnesses.

Jesus appeared to more than five hundred people following his resurrection. The written eyewitness accounts of the resurrection occurred within ten years of the event. If the resurrection was not true, there would have been plenty of eyewitnesses to rebuke the written testimony. But in fact, no record exists of anyone attempting to discredit any of the accounts.

Point 8: Peter's speech at Pentecost.

Now consider Peter's speech at Pentecost, just fifty days after the resurrection, where he addressed the crowd in Jerusalem concerning the life, death, and resurrection of Jesus, which they themselves had witnessed. It is recorded in the book of Acts 2:14–41. Peter reached out to the people, saying:

> Men of Israel, listen to this: Jesus of Nazareth was a man accredited by God to you by miracles, wonders and signs, which God did among you through him, as you yourselves know. This man was handed over to you by God's set purpose and foreknowledge; and you, with the help of wicked men, put him to death by nailing him to the cross. But God raised him from the dead, freeing him from the agony of

> death, because it was impossible for death to keep its hold on him. (Acts 2:22–24)

With this and the rest of the passage, Peter reasoned with the people who saw everything for themselves that:

1. They witnessed Jesus performing miracles, wonders, and signs from God.
2. They knew Jesus was crucified as part of God's plan.
3. They witnessed Jesus's resurrection from the dead back to life.
4. They knew King David wrote about Jesus's resurrection one thousand years before.

When Peter concluded his speech, the people were cut to the heart, knowing firsthand what the scriptures said about the coming Savior, Jesus, and then witnessing firsthand Jesus for several years, including his resurrection. They asked Peter what they should do, and Peter responded to repent, or turn away from their sinful ways, and be baptized in the name of Jesus Christ for the forgiveness of their sins and the gift of the indwelling Holy Spirit. This is exactly what they did. Three thousand people, upon hearing Peter's words, became baptized followers of Jesus. These three thousand people were contemporaries of Jesus who had firsthand knowledge of him and eyewitnesses to his deeds, including his resurrection. Jerusalem was not a metropolis, and for three thousand people to come forward, each risking death themselves, is a very loud testimony to the validity of the resurrection of Jesus.

Point 9: Saul's conversion to Paul.

The life account of Saul of Tarsus is yet another point of evidence to the credibility of Jesus's resurrection. Saul was a dyed-in-the-wool Jew among Jews. He himself was a Pharisee, part of the Jewish leadership acting to have Jesus crucified. Saul himself prosecuted and assisted in the execution of early Christians. He was there when Stephen became the first martyred Christian by stoning and gave his full support for it. He was fully against the Christian movement and acted to snub out the movement through killing the followers of Jesus.

But Saul himself had an about face while in the process of traveling to Damascus to locate and round up more Christians for persecution. The resurrected Jesus appeared to Saul, and Saul became blinded. Jesus spoke directly to Saul and corrected his theology, causing him to do an about face on his view toward Jesus and the Christian movement. With the aid of others, Saul made his way to Damascus, where he became a baptized believer of the resurrected Jesus and converted from Judaism to Christianity. He would then go by his gentile name, Paul, instead of Jewish name, Saul, as he witnessed primarily to the gentiles.

Paul would become one of the main pillars in the spread of Christianity. He would devote the rest of his life to the movement, surviving beatings, floggings, shipwrecks, imprisonment, and ultimately death for his desire to share the good news concerning Jesus. He would also write a large portion of the New Testament.

Paul's conversion after his firsthand encounter with the resurrected Jesus is yet another point of evidence suggesting its truth.

Point 10: Existence of the Christian church.

The Christian church itself is strong proof the disciples believed Jesus was raised from the dead. The resurrection itself was the foundation for Christianity, and the church sprung up thereafter. If the resurrection did not happen, there is no reasonable explanation for the origin of the Christian faith. The resurrection produced the church; the church did not produce the resurrection. The Christian church remains the largest body of faith in the world to this day.

Point 11: Day of worship, Sunday.

For the Jews, Saturday, or the seventh day of the week, being the Sabbath day of rest, was the most significant day of the week.

When the Christian movement came along, the most significant day switched to being Sunday, or the first day of the week. This was the day when Jesus resurrected from the grave. This is still further evidence something very significant happened on this day.

Point 12: Large instant conversion.

Within just a few years after the resurrection, more than ten thousand Jews became followers of Jesus. Such a large conversion of people from Judaism to Christianity is due in part to the firsthand witnessing of Jesus's life, death, and resurrection. If the resurrection was false, or known to be a fabricated story, this large of a conversion would have been unlikely.

Point 13: External written evidence.

There are many non-Christian historical documents, as we will examine in much greater depth in the next chapter, describing Jesus's life, death, and resurrection exactly as it appears in the Bible. In fact, these non-Christian and unfavorable writings toward Christianity give a complete account of the major tenants of the life of Jesus and the Christian faith, including the resurrection of Jesus. Here are just two examples from non-Christian sources:

Historian Phlegon as referenced by Origen:

> Jesus, while alive, was of no assistance to himself, but that he arose after death, and exhibited the marks of his punishment, and showed how his hands had been pierced by nails. (Origen Against Celsus, Book 2, Chapter 59)[2]

Titus Flavius Josephus:

> Now there was about this time Jesus, a wise man if it be lawful to call him a man, for he was a doer of wonders, a teacher of such men as receive the

> truth with pleasure. He drew many after him both of the Jews and the gentiles. He was the Christ. When Pilate, at the suggestion of the principal men among us, had condemned him to the cross, those that loved him at the first did not forsake him, for he appeared to them alive again the third day, as the divine prophets had foretold these and then thousand other wonderful things about him, and the tribe of Christians, so named from him, are not extinct to this day.[3]

So not only are there multiple written accounts of the resurrection within the Bible, but there are multiple external accounts giving full support to the biblical accounts as well.

Point 14: The Bible.

Finally, the Bible clearly supports the resurrection of Jesus from the grave. Previously we have looked at the evidence supporting the geographical, historical, and scientific accuracy of the Bible. The resurrection is just another historical event the Bible gives an accurate account of. The resurrection account can be found in Matthew chapter 28, Mark chapter 16, Luke chapter 24, and John chapter 20. Let's look at the account in the gospel of Mark since it is considered the earliest of the gospels:

> When the Sabbath was over, Mary Magdalene, Mary the mother of James, and Salome bought spices so that they might go to anoint Jesus' body. Very early on the first day of the week, just after sunrise, they were on their way to the tomb and they asked each other, "Who will roll the stone way from the entrance to the tomb?" But when they looked up, they saw the stone, which was very large, had been rolled away. As they entered the tomb, they

> saw a young man dressed in a white robe sitting on the right side, and they were alarmed. "Don't be alarmed," he said, "You are looking for Jesus the Nazarene, who was crucified. He has risen! He is not here. See the place where they laid him. But go, tell his disciples and Peter, "He is going ahead of you into Galilee. There you will see him, just as he told you." (Mark 16:1–7)

Further support of the resurrection is found throughout the New Testament among the multiple authors. Here are just several of these places:

> Therefore it is necessary to choose one of the men who have been with us the whole time the Lord Jesus went in and out among us, beginning from John's baptism to the time when Jesus was taken up from us. For one of these must become a witness with us of his resurrection. (Act 1:21–22)

> And who through the Spirit of holiness was declared with power to be the Son of God by his resurrection from the dead: Jesus Christ our Lord. (Romans 1:4)

> For since death came through a man, the resurrection of the dead comes also through a man. For as in Adam all die, so in Christ all will be made alive. (1 Corinthians 15:21–22)

> I want to know Christ and the power of his resurrection and the fellowship of sharing in his sufferings, becoming like him in his death, and so, somehow, to attain to the resurrection from the dead. (Philippians 3:10–11)

> In it only a few people, eight in all, were saved through water, and this water symbolizes baptism that now saves you also—not the removal of dirt from the body but the pledge of a good conscience toward God. It saves you by the resurrection of Jesus Christ. (1 Peter 3:21)

Now consider Jesus's own testimony concerning himself. The first instance is a dialogue Jesus has with Nicodemus, who was a Pharisee—the very Pharisees who would stir up the crowd in Jerusalem to have Jesus crucified. But Nicodemus privately went to Jesus with a sense of reverence and asked him about eternal life. Here is an abbreviated account from the Bible of that dialogue:

> Now there was a man of the Pharisees named Nicodemus, a member of the Jewish ruling council. He came to Jesus at night and said, "Rabbi, we know you are a teacher who has come from God. For no one could perform the miraculous signs you are doing if God were not with him." In reply Jesus declared, "I tell you the truth, no one can see the kingdom of God unless he is born again." "How can a man be born when he is old?" Nicodemus asked. "Surely he cannot enter a second time into his mother's womb to be born!" Jesus answered, "I tell you the truth, no one can enter the kingdom of God unless he is born of water and the Spirit. Flesh gives birth to flesh, but the Spirit gives birth to spirit." (John 3:1–6)

Jesus speaking to Nicodemus:

> "For God so loved the world that he gave his one and only Son, that whoever believes in him shall not perish but have eternal life. For God did not

> send his Son into the world to condemn the world, but to save the world through him." (John 3:16–17)

What Jesus was describing to Nicodemus was that he was the prophesied Christ who was to come who would take away the sins of the world. And through our faith in Christ, we can have our sins atoned for and have eternal life in heaven.

But it was Peter, the bold disciple, who first put all the pieces together and with the guidance of the Holy Spirit, understood Jesus was the Christ. Here is the account:

> When Jesus came to the region of Caesarea Philippi, he asked his disciples, "Who do people say the Son of Man is?" They replied, "Some say John the Baptist; others say Elijah; and still others, Jeremiah or one of the prophets." "But what about you?" He asked. "Who do you say I am?" Simon Peter answered, "You are the Christ, the Son of the living God." Jesus replied, "Blessed are you, Simon son of Jonah, for this was not revealed to you by man, but by my Father in heaven." (Matthew 16:13–17)

The name *Jesus* means "savior," whereas the name *Christ* means "anointed." So in calling Jesus, "the Christ, the Son of the living God," Peter is proclaiming Jesus is the anointed Savior who was prophesied in the Old Testament and has come into the world. But bold as he was, Peter denied even knowing Jesus three times on the morning of Jesus's crucifixion for fear of his own life. However, after Jesus's resurrection, Peter became emboldened to the point of giving his life to spread the good news about Jesus. Clearly Peter would have known whether the resurrection was true or not, and his life after the event clearly speaks volumes as he was fully a believer and follower of Jesus. The resurrection of Jesus was the defining moment when Peter went from curious follower to sold-out believer. Coincidence?

Chapter 11

What Have Others Written about Jesus?

AD 52 to AD 140

My graduate studies culminated with an oral defense of my thesis. During the exam my major professor and a couple other professors from the department and university could ask me anything they wanted concerning my thesis or my education in general, and it was my job to answer their questions satisfactorily. My degree was on the line based on their collective decision of whether to pass or fail me following this examination. The process can be intense and nerve-racking.

One of my professors, who was a devout Christian, pulled back the oral defense curtain a bit and let me know one of the questions he liked to ask his engineering students during their oral exam. He would ask them a very simple question involving a very well-known equation. He would simply ask them to derive Newton's second law of motion, force equals mass time acceleration, or $F = ma$. Under the pressure of the examination, some students would not think clearly and would quickly write the equation on the chalkboard as if it could be derived. Then they would stare at it and consider each term individually. Turning to acceleration, they knew this was the first time derivative of velocity and also the second time derivative of position, so they would write down the appropriate derivative equations. But at that point they would be stuck. There was nothing else in this equation that can be broken down into more fundamental terms.

After letting the student ponder on this for a bit, my professor told me he would point out to them the equation cannot be derived. It is an observed relationship in the natural world around us. His point was to get the students to realize all of engineering is simply based on observations about the world around us. There is nothing absolute in science itself. Our knowledge is but a very small sliver of the created universe and life itself. In doing this he was trying to remove their biased thought that everything in the world can be explained through scientific principles and to get them to think outside the box and open their minds to the possibility of God.

This is where we are headed in this chapter in our study of Jesus. We want to look outside the box and look at written evidence of Jesus outside the Bible.

Jesus is the focal point of the whole Bible. All sections of the Bible, from the first book to the last, attest to the fact Jesus is the Christ, the anointed Savior of the world. In this regard, the two main sections of the Bible, the Old and New Testament, are like a patient going to the doctor for an ailment. The doctor takes most of the time to examine the patient to determine what is wrong. Once the doctor knows the problem, the prescribed cure generally takes much less time to administer. Likewise, the much longer of the two main sections of the Bible, the Old Testament, diagnoses and points out the problem with humankind, sin. The much shorter New Testament introduces the cure for sin, Jesus.

It's worth pointing out the Bible is not a single book. It is more like a set of encyclopedias with multiple authors. The Bible is composed of sixty-six different books, written by over forty authors, over fifteen hundred years on three continents and using three languages. It is not a single source or piece of written evidence; it is forty separate witnesses attesting to Jesus. Further, the Bible was written during a period when eyewitnesses were still alive who knew the truth. There is no evidence any of these eyewitnesses refuted what is written in the Bible concerning Jesus. Not one.

All forty authors of the Bible directly or indirectly attest to Jesus through their writings. All eight authors in the New Testament refer to Jesus by name: Matthew, Mark, Luke, John, Jude, Peter, James, and Paul. All eight people either knew Jesus personally or were close companions to one of Jesus's disciples who knew him personally. Before we move on to the external sources, it is worth a moment to hear a bit of what these various writers wrote concerning Jesus, or a snippet of what they recorded Jesus himself saying:

Mark: Date of Writing: Early 50s AD

The general consensus is that the gospel of Mark was written by John Mark, who was a close companion of one of the twelve disciples, Peter. Jesus speaking:

> If anyone would come after me, he must deny himself and take up his cross and follow me. For whoever wants to save his life will lose it, but whoever loses his life for me and for the gospel will save it. (Mark 8:34–35)

Paul: Date of Writing: AD 55

Paul was a Jewish Pharisee, a religious leader, who originally persecuted Christians by putting them to death. Paul, whose original name was Saul, had a direct encounter with the risen Christ Jesus as he was traveling to Damascus to round up more Christians to persecute. Following his encounter, he became a baptized believer and then spent the rest of his life spreading the good news concerning Jesus to the gentiles (anyone who was not a Jew) despite beatings and imprisonments for doing so. Paul was martyred for his faith around AD 68. Paul gives us an account of what Jesus said in the Upper Room the night before Jesus's crucifixion when he instituted communion, which is practiced to this day by the Christian church:

> The Lord Jesus, on the night he was betrayed, took bread, and when he had given thanks, he broke it and said, "This is my body, which is for you; do this in remembrance of me." In the same way, after supper he took the cup saying, "This cup is the new covenant in my blood; do this, whenever you drink it, in remembrance of me." (1 Corinthians 11:23–25)

Matthew: Date of Writing: Late 50s AD

Matthew was one of the twelve disciples, or apostles, of Jesus. He was a tax collector who put his work aside to follow Jesus. In the gospels of Mark and Luke he is referred to by his other name, Levi. Jesus said:

> For if you forgive men when they sin against you, your heavenly Father will also forgive you. But if you do not forgive men their sins, your Father will not forgive your sins. (Matthew 6:14–15)

Luke: Date of Writing: AD 59-63

The gospel of Luke is attributed to the physician Luke, who wrote the books of both Luke and Acts. He was a companion of Paul during his missionary journeys to spread the good news concerning Jesus. Jesus said:

> It is not the healthy who need a doctor, but the sick. I have not come to call the righteous, but sinners to repentance. (Luke 5:31)

James: Date of Writing: Early 60s AD

James was a younger brother of Jesus and became the leader of the Jerusalem council. At first, James was not a follower of Jesus but then became a devout follower after Jesus's resurrection. James was martyred for his faith around AD 62. James opens his book with the following:

> James, a servant of God and of the Lord Jesus Christ. (James 1:1)

Peter: Date of Writing: Early 60s AD

Peter was one of the twelve disciples who was known for his boldness. It was Peter who briefly walked on water with Jesus. Peter was the first person who recognized Jesus is the Christ prophesied in the Old Testament. Peter gave his life spreading the good news of Jesus following the resurrection. Referring to Jesus he states:

> For you know that it was not with perishable things such as silver or gold that you were redeemed from the empty way of life handed down to you from your forefathers, but with the precious blood of Christ, a lamb without blemish or defect. (1 Peter 1:18–19)

Jude: Date of Writing: AD 65

The author of Jude was either Judas (Greek form of Judah, or Jude) or Jesus's brother, Judas. In either case, he personally knew Jesus well. Judas does not quote Jesus directly but gives us this commentary:

> Keep yourselves in God's love as you wait for the mercy of our Lord Jesus Christ to bring you to eternal life. (Jude 21)

John: Date of Writing: Prior to AD 70

John was the beloved disciple of Jesus who traveled at Jesus's side for three years. John was a close friend and follower of Jesus. John wrote the gospel John, 1 John, 2 John, 3 John, and Revelation. Jesus said:

> A new command I give you: Love one another. As I have loved you, so you must love one another. By this all men will know that you are my disciples if you love one another. (John 13:34–35)

Although the evidence examined throughout this book so far is mostly in direct support of the Bible, and Jesus is the focal point of the Bible, there are also sources outside of the Bible validating Jesus. There are in fact dozens of ancient, nonbiblical written documents validating Jesus's life, death, and resurrection just as revealed in the Bible. These ancient writings span the entire spectrum from favorable, or pro-Christianity, to unfavorable, or anti-Christianity.

First, let's look at a list of some of the ancient sources referring to Jesus that are favorable to Christianity. This list would include Clement of Rome, 2 Clement, Ignatius of Antioch, Polycarp's letter to Philippians, martyrdom of Polycarp, Didache, letter to Barnabus, Shepherd of Hermas, fragments of Papias, letter of Diognetus, Epistula Apostolorum, Heggisipus, Justyn Martyr, Aristides, Athenagoras, Theophilus of Antioch, Quadratus, Aristo of Pella, and Melito of Sardis. Further, there are five more written documents mentioning Jesus portraying themselves as Christian writings, but they are not generally accepted as authentic, God-inspired Christian writings. These include Second Treatise of Seth, Gnostic Gospel of

Thomas, Apocryphon of John, Gospel of Truth, and Apocalypse of Peter.

Turning now to ancient, unfavorable or anti-Christianity documents, there are many writers and sources who mention Jesus. To raise the bar in our examination of the evidence, however, we will limit our study to unfavorable or anti-Christianity sources written within roughly one hundred years of the resurrection. From pagan and secular authors this list includes historian Thallus, historian Titus Flavius Josephus, Roman politician Pliny the Younger, Roman historian Cornelius Tacitus, historian Suetonius, Greek satirist Lucian, and historian Phelgon. Further, we have the pro-Judaism, anti-Christianity writings from the Jews called the Talmud.

Let's examine these writings to see what they have to say concerning Jesus:

Thallas: Date of Writing: AD 52

The writings of Thallus, an early Greek historian, are so old that his original writings no longer exist. We learn what he wrote from fragments of other writers who quote him. One such writer is Julius Africanus, who, writing around AD 221, quotes Thallus regarding the darkness occurring at Jesus's crucifixion:

> This darkness Thallus, in the third book of his History, calls, as appear to me without reason, an eclipse of the sun. For the Hebrews celebrate the Passover on the 14th day according to the moon, and the passion of our Saviour falls on the day before the Passover; but an eclipse of the sun takes place only when the moon comes under the sun. And it cannot happen at any other time but in the interval between the first day of the new moon and the last of the old, that is, at their junction: how then should an eclipse be supposed to happen

> when the moon is almost diametrically opposite the sun? Let that opinion pass however; let it carry the majority with it; and let this portent of the world be deemed an eclipse of the sun, like others portent only to the eye. Phelgon records that, in the time of Tiberius Caesar, at full moon, there was a full eclipse of the sun from the sixth hour to the nine—manifestly that one of which we speak.
> Julius Africanus, Chronography, 18:1[1]

Titus Flavius Josephus: Date of Writing: AD 93

Josephus, a Jew, was born a few years after Jesus's crucifixion. From a priestly line, he himself became a Pharisee at the age of nineteen. He was a historian who wrote under the rule of Roman emperor Vespasian. Consequently, being a Pharisee, he would have been unfavorable to Christianity, and being under the eye of Roman authority, he was careful not to offend the Romans. In his writings on the history of the Jews, *Antiquities of the Jews* in AD 93, he wrote three separate accounts about Christians. The following is his description of Jesus as we looked at in the previous chapter on the resurrection:

> Now there was about this time Jesus, a wise man if it be lawful to call him a man, for he was a doer of wonders, a teacher of such men as receive the truth with pleasure. He drew many after him both of the Jews and the gentiles. He was the Christ. When Pilate, at the suggestion of the principal men among us, had condemned him to the cross, those that loved him at the first did not forsake him, for he appeared to them alive again the third day, as the divine prophets had foretold these and then thousand other wonderful things about him, and

> the tribe of Christians, so named from him, are not extinct to this day.[2]

Writing in the same AD 93 timeframe, Josephus refers to Jesus as the brother of James who was martyred by stoning in AD 62. In his *Antiquities of the Jews*, book 20, chapter 9, he refers to the actions of the high priest Ananias against James:

> But the younger Ananus who, as we said, received the high priesthood, was of a bold disposition and exceptionally daring; he followed the party of the Sadducees, who are severe in judgment above all the Jews, as we have already shown. As therefore Ananus was of such a disposition, he thought he had now a good opportunity, as Festus was now dead, and Albinus was still on the road; so he assembled a council of judges, and brought before it the brother of Jesus the so-called Christ, whose name was James, together with some others, and having accused them as law-breakers, he delivered them over to be stoned.[3]

Jewish Talmud: Date of Original Writings: AD 100

The Jews shared a large amount of information orally from generation to generation. Starting around AD 70, this information was written down by Rabbi Akiba and then later edited by Rabbi Meir. Then around AD 200, Rabbi Judah completed the writings. This compilation of writings along with their ancient commentaries are known as the Talmud.

It is believed among scholars that various Talmudic writings refer to Jesus using code words. But examining only passages where it is very clear Jesus of the Bible is being referred to, we see the following:

> Jesus practiced magic and led Israel astray. (b. Sanhedrin 43a; cf. t. Shabbat 11.15; b. Shabbat 104b)[4]

> Rabbi Hisda (d. 309) said that Rabbi Jeremiah bar Abba said, 'What is that which is written, 'No evil will befall you, nor shall any plague come near your house'? (Psalm 91:10) … 'No evil will befall you' (means) that evil dreams and evil thoughts will not tempt you; 'nor shall any plague come near your house' (means) that you will not have a son or a disciple who burns his food like Jesus of Nazareth. (b. Sanhedrin 103a; cf. b. Berakhot 17b)[5]

> It was taught: On the day before the Passover they hanged Jesus. A herald went before him for forty days (proclaiming), "He will be stoned, because he practiced magic and enticed Israel to go astray. Let anyone who knows anything in his favor come forward and plead for him." But nothing was found in his favor, and they hanged him on the day before the Passover. (b. Sanhedrin 43a)[6]

Pliny the Younger: Date of Writing: AD 112

Pliny was a Roman author and administrator, who served as the governor of Bithynia in Asia Minor under Emperor Trajan, is best known for his letters. In one of his letters to the emperor, dated around AD 112, he describes the early Christians and their worship practices:

> They (the Christians) were in the habit of meeting on a certain fixed day before it was light, when they sang in alternate verses a hymn to Christ, as to a god, and bound themselves by a solemn oath,

> not to any wicked deeds, but never to commit any fraud, theft or adultery, never to falsify their word, nor deny a trust when they should be called upon to deliver it up; after which it was their custom to separate, and then reassemble to partake of food—but food of an ordinary and innocent kind.[7]

In another writing dated a year later:

> Even this practice, however, they had abandoned after the publication of my edict, by which, according to your orders, I had forbidden political associations. I therefore judged it so much more the necessary to extract the real truth, with the assistance of torture, from two female slaves, who were styled deaconesses: but I could discover nothing more than depraved and excessive superstition.
>
> In the meanwhile, the method I have observed towards those who have denounced to me as Christians is this: I interrogated them whether they were Christians; if they confessed it I repeated the question twice again, adding the threat of capital punishment; if they still persevered, I ordered them to be executed. For whatever the nature of their creed might be, I could at least feel no doubt that contumacy and inflexible obstinacy deserved chastisement. There were others possessed of the same folly; but because they were Roman citizens, I signed an order for them to be transferred to Rome.[8]

Cornelius Tacitus: Date of Writing: AD 116

Cornelius Tacitus was a Roman historian and is considered one of the most trusted and accurate historians of ancient Rome. He authored both the *Annals* that covered from AD 14 to AD 68, and the "Histories" covering from AD 68 to AD 96, the period that covered Jesus's ministry and the growth of the Christian Church. Although he mentions Christ and Christianity in his writings elsewhere, the most important one is found in *Annals,* where he describes the great fire in Rome in AD 64 and Emperor Nero blaming Christians:

> Consequently, to get rid of the report, Nero fastened the guilt and inflicted the most exquisite tortures on a class hated for their abominations, called Christians by the populace. Christus, from whom the name had its origin, suffered the extreme penalty during the reign of Tiberius at the hands of one of our procurators, Pontius Pilate, and a most mischievous superstition, thus checked for the moment, again broke out not only in Judea, the source of the evil, but even in Rome, where all things hideous and shameful from every part of the world find their centre and become popular. Accordingly, as arrest was first made of all who pleaded guilty; then, upon their information, an immense multitude was convicted, not so much of the crime of firing the city, as of hatred against humankind. Mockery of every sort was added to their deaths. Covered with the skins of beasts, they were torn by dogs and perished, or were nailed to crosses, or were doomed to the flames and burnt, to serve as a nightly illumination, when daylight had expired.[9]

Gaius Suetonius Tranquillas: Date of Writing: AD 120

Gaius Suetonius Tranquillas, or better known just as Suetonius, was chief secretary to Emperor Hadrian and a Roman historian. Through his writings he confirmed the report found in the Bible in Acts 18:2 that Emperor Claudius expelled the Christians from Rome in AD 49:

> Because the Jews at Rome caused constant disturbances at the instigation of Chrestus (Christ), he (Claudius) expelled them from the city (Rome). (Life of Claudius, 25:4)[10]

In another, he confirmed other writings concerning the great fire in Rome in 64 AD and Nero blaming and severely punishing the Christians:

> Nero inflicted punishment on the Christians, a sect given to a new and mischievous religious belief. (Lives of the Caesars, 26.2)[11]

Lucian of Samosata: Date of Writing: AD 120
Lucian was a second-century Greek satirist who wrote sarcastically and critically of Christ and Christians. Ironically by doing this, he provided additional support and evidence Christ and Christians were exactly as described in the Bible:

> The Christians, you know, worship a man to this day—the distinguished personage who introduced their novel rites, and was crucified on that account….You see, these misguided creatures start with the general conviction that they are immortal for all time, which explains the contempt of death and voluntary self-devotion which are so common among them; and then it was impressed on them by their original lawgiver that they are all brothers, from the moment that they are converted, and deny the gods of Greece, and worship the crucified sage, and live after his laws. All this they take quite on faith, with the result that they despise all worldly goods alike, regarding them merely as common property. (Lucian, The Death of Peregrine. 11–13)[12]

Phelgon of Tralles: Date of Writing: AD 140

Phelgon was a Greek writer and freedman of Emperor Hadrian. Like the early Greek writer Thallus, Phelgon's original writings are no longer in existence, and we need to rely on other ancient writers, Julius Africanus and Origen, who reference Phelgon's writings. In his writings, Phelgon describes the darkness during Jesus's crucifixion:

> Phlegon records that, in the time of Tiberius Caesar, at full moon, there was a full eclipse of the sun from the sixth to the ninth hour. (Africanus, Chronography, 18:1)[13]

Phlegon, as mentioned by Origen (an early church theologian and scholar):

> Now Phlegon, in the thirteenth or fourteenth book, I think, of his Chronicles, not only ascribed to Jesus a knowledge of future events… but also testified that the result corresponded to His predictions. (Origen Against Celsus, Book 2, Chapter 14)[14]

> And with regard to the eclipse in the time of Tiberius Caesar, in whose reign Jesus appears to have been crucified, and the great earthquakes which then took place. (Origen Against Celsus, Book 2, Chapter 33)[15]

> Jesus, while alive, was of no assistance to himself, but that he arose after death, and exhibited the marks of his punishment, and showed how his hands had been pierced by nails. (Origen Against Celsus, Book 2, Chapter 59)[16]

So, putting it all together and comparing what we know about the major tenants of Jesus from both the Bible and unfavorable, or anti-Christian, sources written within roughly 100 years of the resurrection, we arrive at the following:

	Source of Information	
	Bible	External
Jesus was a real person.	√	√
Jesus was a wise teacher.	√	√
Jesus was a leader.	√	√
Jesus's teachings lived on.	√	√
Jesus drew both Jews and gentiles to Him.	√	√
Jesus led the Jews away from their beliefs.	√	√
Jesus had magical powers.	√	√
Jesus performed miraculous deeds.	√	√
Jesus accurately predicted future events.	√	√
Jesus's crucifixion was brought about by the Jews.	√	√
Jesus was crucified during the time of Tiberius Caesar.	√	√
Jesus was crucified on the eve of the Jewish Passover.	√	√
Jesus was crucified under the direction of Pontius Pilate.	√	√
Jesus was hung and crucified on a wooden cross.	√	√
Jesus's crucifixion had darkness from sixth to ninth hour.	√	√
Jesus's crucifixion accompanied by earthquake.	√	√
Jesus appeared alive again the third day after his death.	√	√

Jesus's resurrection on the third day was prophesied.	√	√
Jesus showed his wounds after his resurrection.	√	√
Jesus's followers met on a certain fixed day (Sunday).	√	√
Jesus's disciples and followers upheld a high moral code.	√	√
Jesus's followers held to their faith in the face of death.	√	√
Jesus's brother James was martyred.	√	√
Jesus was worshiped as God.	√	√
Jesus was the Christ.	√	√

In essence, if we did not have a Bible and only relied on ancient non-Christian or anti-Christian documents written within roughly one hundred years of the resurrection, we would essentially know all major aspects of Jesus's life, including his death and resurrection, just as from the Bible. Considering the scarcity of written documents during this timeframe, this is remarkable. Just as the Bible has been proven to be an accurate, trustworthy source for people, places, and events, the life of Jesus is just another accurate historical account. The written evidence outside the box concerning Jesus aligns exactly with the Bible. Coincidence?

Chapter 12

Is Jesus the Christ?

I have yet to meet a totally unbiased person, myself included. Over time the lens we view the world through develops filters and we start to see things not as they truly are, but as our preconceived, biased filters see things.

As an engineer, it became laughably apparent to me how polarizing these filters can be to an otherwise objective person. On one particular project, our product was selected over worldwide competition by one of our customers for use in their system. However, months after we had been sourced, they raised the objection that our product was too noisy, and the magnetic noise had to be reduced or they would source the business to one of our competitors. Urgent meetings were called, and I found myself being whisked away to one of their test facilities to hear their objection firsthand.

Our customer had predetermined we would do an A to B type subjective test where they would put a competitor's product in their system and we would listen to the noise. Then they would put our product into their system and listen to the noise again. Overseeing the testing and driving the project was an up-and-coming engineering manager in this company. From her initial greeting to her gruff attitude, it was apparent her mind was made up and she was out to displace our product with our competitor's product.

So the testing ensued. First the competitor's product was put in the system, and we quietly listened to the noise as the system was put through its operating range. Audible magnetic noise could be heard, but there was nothing that seemed exceptional, one way or the other, with its noise characteristics. Next, the competitor's product was removed, and our product was put in the exact same system. The system was again put through its operating range as before. Moments after the testing started, the manager put her hands over her ears as if to protect them and complained wildly about the excessive magnetic noise. To my ears, not only did I not hear loud magnetic noise; I didn't hear any magnetic noise at all. The other participants in the evaluation were somewhat neutral as they apparently did not want to go against their manager.

The lid covering the system was lifted as the technician prepared to remove our product and replace it again with our competitor's product for another A to B evaluation. When he lifted the lid, I spotted something that hit my engineering funny bone, and I could not help myself; I started to laugh. The manager asked what was wrong, and I said "Look, the electrical connector going to our product was not connected during the test. Our product wasn't even running during the test. It couldn't have produced *any* magnetic noise during the test!"

Her bias was as obvious as her embarrassed red face. Her mind was so determined our product was noisy that she could not be objective. In fact, her biased mind overwrote what her ears were actually telling her. It was a real-life example of, "Don't confuse me with the facts; my mind is made up."

So how about you? Can you put your biases aside and examine the facts and evidence with an open, objective mind? Or will pride or arrogance get in the way of you reaching the most important decision in your life, which is whether Jesus is the Christ, the Savior of the world? I invite you to reflect on the material presented in this book and then form your own unbiased opinion.

How Did It All Begin?

The Bible has been steadfast through the years in what is states. In fact, it has not changed since its initial writing starting thirty-five hundred years ago. The Dead Sea Scrolls gave us great evidence in this regard since its Old Testament scrolls are dated to a couple hundred years before Jesus's birth. When compared to scrolls used to construct the King James Version of the Bible in 1611, they were virtually word for word. At the very start of the Bible in the book of Genesis, the Bible clearly states there was a definite beginning to the universe, and it was God who created it.

Science, however, has evolved in its understanding of the origins of the universe. Until as recently as the twentieth century, it was felt the heavens were eternal and static. They always were and will always be. This changed when Einstein applied his general theory of relativity to the whole universe. The results implied the universe had a beginning, and a beginning implied a creator. He circumvented this possibility by artificially adding a "cosmological constant" into his equations to predict a static, eternal universe in line with his atheist beliefs. Colleagues throughout the world challenged his assumption based on their own studies and observations. After peering through Edwin Hubble's telescope in Pasadena, California, in 1931, Einstein observed the universe was expanding virtually at the speed of light. This caused him to rethink his conclusions, and he eliminated his biasing factor and concluded the universe had a beginning and there must be a creator, whom he believed existed.

So even though we sometimes take science as the ultimate truth, in reality science is just people's observations of the created world around them. Sometimes we get it right, or so we think, and sometimes we do not. Science, though, generally self-corrects, and as more data becomes available and analyzed, our understanding of the truth draws closer to the ultimate truth. In the case of the universe, the universally accepted understanding is everything came into being per the big bang theory.

So what? Approximately thirty-five hundred years ago Moses

recorded in the book of Genesis of the Bible an accurate description of the origin of the universe that is in full agreement with the big bang, something no other book can claim. Coincidence?

Creating the Perfect Biosphere for Life

After Moses's description of the beginning of the universe in Genesis, he goes on to describe how God created the billions of planets and in scientific detail the creation of earth. His description and order of events fits our current scientific understanding perfectly.

Further, the precision of various life-enabling factors is startling. The relative mass and charges of the neutrons, protons, and electrons composing nature's smallest building blocks, atoms, is astounding. With just extremely small variations in these values, atoms could not exist. Or consider the resonance of carbon. It is fine tuned to extreme precision as well. Just an extremely little higher or lower and carbon does not exist, and if carbon does not exist, we do not exist.

On the other side of the size scale, the universe itself is finely balanced to enable life to exist on earth. Gravitational forces are balanced on a razor's edge to enable the universe and earth to exist. Our sun is just the right size to provide a moderate climate and for liquid water to exist on its surface. Our moon is necessary to stabilize our tilt and provide moderate climates as well as to generate circulation in our oceans, which acts like a giant thermal buffer moderating climate as well. Our galaxy type is just the right type to permit a circular orbit of our solar system in a safe zone.

So what? The extreme fine tuning of the world around us, from the smallest to the largest, points toward purposeful design and an intelligent designer. The Bible describes how it was God who created these ecosystems, and his description aligns with our current scientific understanding. Coincidence?

How Did Life Begin?

After the environmental conditions are just right for the existence of animal life, life appears on the earth as described in days 5 and

6 in the Bible. Again, it is right in line with our current scientific understanding of how life rolled out.

With all our sophisticated science and technology, the creation of life from nonlife is still a miracle. We do not know how to take lifeless atoms and molecules and create a living organism out of them. It truly is a miracle.

Once there is a living organism to begin with, Darwin created a theory whereby through genetic mutations and survival of the fittest, different life forms came into existence. Per our current scientific understanding, though, his theory is plagued with problems. First, gene mutations are not beneficial to the host organism. Mutations cause deformities and sickness in the host organism, and when compounded over succeeding generations, it will lead to the extinction of the species. We are observing this now with the human race. Gene mutations are the root of a whole host of medical issues, such as cancer, and with sufficient future generations and increased levels of mutations, they could eventually cause the extinction of humankind. For Darwin's theory to be correct, mutations must lead to an improvement in the species, but in fact, they do not.

The second challenge with Darwinism is it is simply not supported in the fossil record. For evolution to be true, there must be a multitude of transitional species in the fossil record as species evolved over long periods of time. What the fossil record reveals, however, is a huge burst of different life forms, in a biological instant, during the Cambrian Explosion. One moment there are only single-celled bacteria, and the next moment there are a variety of complex life forms. This simply cannot happen if the theory of evolution were true.

So what? Once again, the Bible gives an accurate scientific account and roll out of how various life forms came to be at the hand of a creator God. Coincidence?

Are We Physically Evolved Apes?

The Bible states humankind is the crowning creation of God. Humans were the last of the created beings, and God's intent is for humans to rule over the rest of the created world. Per the Bible, humankind did not evolve from a common lineage with monkey and apes who are of a different "kind."

So what is the latest from science? First, we have already looked at the fallacy of Darwinism and the theory of evolution that simply is not supported with scientific data. In addition, there are no transitional species in the fossil record connecting a knuckle-walking ape to an upright-walking human. We have monkeys and apes and we have humans, and that is it.

But recently we became the beneficiaries of human genome studies that have really shed light on the origin of humankind. Researchers were surprised when different people groups from around the world had virtually the same DNA with very little differences. This indicates a relatively young age for humankind. How young? By studying the gene mutation rate, the age of humankind has been back calculated. When this is done, multiple recent studies suggest humankind is approximately only six thousand years old, exactly in accordance with what the Bible indicates. Further, this young age for the history of humankind eliminates any possibility of humans evolving from apes, again just as the Bible states. Coincidence?

Are We Spiritually Evolved Apes?

The Bible indicates humans are different from animals since they have eternal souls, *neshamas*. In fact, the central theme of the Bible is by placing our faith in Jesus, our sins will be forgiven by God and our eternal soul will reside in heaven with him. An eternal soul, separate from the physical body, cannot exist in a physical worldview and simply does not make sense.

So what does science say? Again, science is not the source of ultimate truth, but it is a good screen for evaluating data and the basis for forming opinions. One of the first refutations to a purely physical world is the idea of thought itself. How could physical atoms and molecules have thought? How does a single-celled bacteria evolve to have the intelligence of modern humans?

Next, humans have a sense of morality. Again, apart from a creator God who coded it into us, where does it come from? How can molecules on their own develop a sense of right and wrong that is universal across all humankind?

Another indication of something beyond the physical comes from the thousands of near-death experiences. In a medically dead condition, some survivors have been able to vividly recount details and perspectives that could only come from an alive person.

Finally, human culture is an indication of humankind's spirituality. Humankind stands alone in terms of culture. Nothing is even a very distant second. So when did humankind's culture spring into being, which also indicates when humankind itself came into being? Around six thousand years ago, exactly as the Bible indicates for the dawn of humankind. Coincidence?

What Yom Is It?

The order of events of the creation of the universe and all the life forms as stated in the Bible is in accordance with modern science. However, some have looked at the six days for creation listed in the Bible and scoffed at it in light of science's aging of the various events.

Central to this discussion is the interpretation of the original Hebrew word *yom* appearing in the Bible and the location of the "clock" during this time. As discussed, yom has multiple meanings, just as the word *day* does, such as "back in the day." If yom is interpreted as a lengthy but finite period of time, then yoms one through six fit our current understanding of aging the creation period perfectly. Further, if the "clock" is located where it reflects a universal time, then with time dilation from the theory of relativity, the timing of the six days of creation also collapse neatly, and exactly, into six consistent periods of time. Either way, or both, the Bible gives an accurate account of creation events and timing per modern scientific dating of the universe, the earth, and life itself. Coincidence?

Old Testament–Era Evidence

The Bible is full of people, places, dates, and events. Yet not one single piece of the thousands of archeological artifacts unearthed or discovered has ever refuted the Bible. Not one. The Bible has been proven to be a historical and geographical accurate account again and again. The evidence presented and discussed in this chapter is just a small portion of the material backing this statement. Serious scholars, whether Christians or not, do not question the impeccable trustworthiness of the Bible in describing people, places, and events.

What about seemingly outlandish events, such as Noah's ark and the flood? As shown, there is solid scientific data indicating the world was once flooded, and a wooden structure of some sort rests high atop Mount Ararat in modern Turkey, where the Bible indicates the ark came to rest. Further, modern human genome studies indicate a population bottleneck in humankind's recent past and a female lineage split into three lines. This is consistent with the flood and Noah's three daughters-in-law who were aboard the ark who would have yielded three distinct lineages. Coincidence?

Prophecies on Jesus

Just as the Bible is full of people, places, and events that have been proven true, the Bible is full of prophecies as well. There are well over one thousand in all, covering people, cities, and nations. Like the historical and geographical accuracy of general events, with the exception of end times prophecies that are to come, these prophecies have been proven accurate and true.

Regarding Jesus specifically, there are over three hundred prophecies alone. Again, all of them have proven to come true, with the exception of end times prophecies, which are in the future. Jesus truly is the Savior of the world the Old Testament prophesied about.

Further, we have Dead Sea Scrolls discovered in the Qumran caves predating Jesus by hundreds of years, so we know the prophecies were not written after the fact but were indeed truly prophecies.

Jesus's fulfillment of these prophecies validates who the Bible says he is and the divine nature of scripture itself. Coincidence?

New Testament–Era Evidence

The New Testament archeological evidence is a continuation of the Old Testament. Hundreds of artifacts indicate the people, places, and events described occurred exactly as they are written. The New Testament has been proven to be a reliable historical document. Every place Jesus visited or traveled to during his ministry on earth can be visited today. Jesus's life, teachings, crucifixion, and resurrection are just additional accurate historical accounts given in the Bible. Coincidence?

Did the Resurrection Really Happen?

We examined the evidence of the resurrection from fourteen different perspectives. The evidence from a variety of different angles strongly supports that the resurrection is another accurate historical fact the Bible records. Among those who would have known the truth, the thousands of eyewitnesses, not one ever came forward to refute any claims of the Bible or other writings concerning the historical account of the resurrection of Jesus. The resurrection is another historically accurate account in the Bible. Coincidence?

What Have Others Written about Jesus?

Imagine for a moment we put aside the sixty-six books of the Bible and the evidence we have indicating the Bible is a trustworthy historical document through the ages from the beginning of time until the first century AD. If we did that, what would we know about Jesus based strictly on other written documents and from viewpoints unfavorable to Christianity? From the variety of writers who were unfavorable toward Christianity, we would know every major tenant and facet of Jesus's life. We would know about his birth, his life, his teachings, his healings, his miracles, his crucifixion, his resurrection, and his ascension. In other words, the written external evidence of Jesus supports every facet of his life the Bible states he did. Coincidence?

Is Jesus the Christ?

So what do you think? Is it numerous coincidences or convincing evidence? Is it mere coincidence that for all the various aspects examined, our scientific knowledge, historical records, and archeological evidence all line up with the Bible and Jesus?

Decades ago when I started my personal quest for the truth concerning Jesus, I was determined to follow the evidence in a scientific fashion, wherever it may lead me. Along the way I spent a lot of time in libraries, long before the days of the Internet, exploring the Bible and Jesus in great detail and from many different aspects. During this process, a very curious phenomenon emerged. Initially, I was using science as my measurement system for truth, sort of a truth gage. If something is an absolute, unchanging, eternal truth, then it should align with scientific thought. Or so I thought. What I discovered is that this science-based "truth gage" is flawed. Through the ages it is constantly being recalibrated. New findings and new understandings in the scientific world continue to alter what is "truth." Sometimes what was once regarded as fact and truth to the scientific community, such as the earth is the center of the universe, or the universe is static, becomes challenged with new findings as our scientific understanding deepens. What came to the forefront again and again is that science is not a source of absolute, unchanging, eternal truth. It changes over time.

Conversely, my studies and investigations into the Bible and Jesus revealed a steadfast, rock-solid, never-changing source of information. The Bible and Jesus have not changed over time, nor have any of the facts or claims concerning them ever been proven wrong or in error. The further and deeper I drilled into them, looking for any cracks in the proverbial armor, the deeper and more solid the evidence became in support of them as sources of eternal truth. In the area of science, particularly in the area of creation, over time science has walked, then jogged, and then sprinted toward what the Bible has been saying all along, and all alone. Science and the Bible are now saying the same thing regarding creation. Verbatim. Sadly, very few people recognize this. Ironically, it is the Bible that has been the truth gage all along concerning creation, not science. Science is just confirming what the Bible has been saying for thousands of years.

Beyond physical science, the Bible has been proven reliable again and again from a historical perspective whenever it discusses people, places, or events. As I prodded into the Bible and Jesus from many perspectives, I would sometimes uncover a small item, such as an apparent small contradiction between the gospels. However, further studies into every single little item has upheld the impeccable truth of the Bible and Jesus. In addition, I have spent many hours reading anti-Christian and atheist-based writings on Christianity looking for any small crack that I might have overlooked. But again and again, I have yet to find anything. What I have concluded is that the Bible, and what it says concerning Jesus, is rock-solid, reliable, accurate, recorded history.

From an intellectual perspective, we can certainly have confidence in the personage and historicity of Jesus, who said and did the various things recorded about him. Now the question facing us becomes a spiritual one: is Jesus really the Christ? Is he truly the Savior of the world, and by repenting of our sins and putting faith in Him, through grace God will forgive our sins and grant us eternal life in heaven? To bolster our faith in this spiritual area, there is strong and clear evidence of divine influence in the writing of the Bible with its hundreds of fulfilled prophecies. How do you explain the multitude of prophecies made hundreds of years in advance, with every single one of them being fulfilled exactly as predicted, without giving credit to a divine influence? Still further, as discussed previously, we have a variety of evidence indicating Jesus really did resurrect from the dead, giving further evidence of divine influence through this miracle. Therefore, there is indeed evidence the Bible and Jesus are much more than physical entities.

The Bible is very clear concerning the significance of putting our faith and trust in Jesus with passages such as the following:

> Whoever believes in the Son has eternal life, but whoever rejects the Son will not see life, for God's wrath remains upon him. (John 3:36)

> For my Father's will is that everyone who looks to the Son and believes in him shall have eternal life, and I will raise him up at the last day. (John 6:40)

> Jesus answered, "I am the way and the truth and the life. No one comes to the Father except through me." (John 16:6)

The Bible is also very clear that God wants us to put our faith in Jesus. It is impossible to please God without faith:

> And without faith it is impossible to please God, because anyone who comes to him must believe that he exists and that he rewards those who earnestly seek him. (Hebrews 11:6)

We tend to think what matters most in life is what can be seen. The information presented in this book is mostly "seen" type of physical evidence. However, what really matters most in life is what is unseen. Ironically, everything seen is temporary and everything unseen is eternal. Someday our faith will be as sight, but for now God desires that we have faith in what we cannot directly see. We long for more than his written word. We long to hear his voice audibly broadcast across loudspeakers. But instead, he often speaks to us in a still, soft, inaudible voice through his Spirit. He can be knocking on the door to our heart right now, but we allow the cares of the world around us to drown out his calling.

In this regard, as stated in the beginning of this book, unlike my engineering world where answers can be physically or mathematically determined, such as through a controlled experiment, issues of the spiritual realm are not as easy to determine. I further asked, how do you run a faith-based experiment involving God? Well, I actually do know of an experiment if you believe Jesus is the Christ and desire to become a follower. Wherever you are, bow your head in prayer to our heavenly Father, asking him to come into your life, you repent of your past sins, and you desire to have a relationship with him through Jesus. If you truly and earnestly believe and pray this, God will answer your prayer and welcome you. I have no doubt.

Why do I have such bold confidence your prayer will be answered? First, everyone I personally know, read about, or heard about who made such a prayer, God has positively responded to them. I know of no exception. From an engineering perspective, the correlation is 100 percent. Second, and even more fundamentally, God will respond to you because he truly loves you.

We were made for eternity, and our souls will live forever. Where we spend eternity is entirely our choice. God has given us free will to choose. We can either embrace God's plan and turn to Jesus in faith, receiving his blessings now and eternal benefits in heaven in the future, or turn away and suffer the eternal consequences in hell. The choice is ours. For now the invitation is open, but someday it will close. No one knows how much time they have here on earth. Our next breath could be our last. And then it's too late. Eternity is a long time to be wrong.

Listen to what the Lord God said to his people centuries ago and also speaks to us today:

> "For I know the plans I have for you," declares the Lord, "plans to prosper you and not to harm you, plans to give you hope and a future. Then you will call upon me and come and pray to me, and I will listen to you. You will see me and find me when you seek me with all your heart." (Jeremiah 29:11–14)

God's knocking. Will you open the door and embrace Christ confidently?

Acknowledgments

An old proverb states that a journey of a thousand miles begins with a single step. Such is the case with the completion of this book that has its roots over two decades ago. I am grateful for the many people along the way whose contributions led to the writing and completion of this book. I am especially indebted to ministers Larry Marshall and Bob Bell at Bethany Christian Church in Anderson, Indiana, who allowed me to take that first single step by allowing me, and encouraging me, to begin sharing this information within the church. Likewise, I want to express my appreciation to ministers Andrew Hodges and Tom Wiles at Fall Creek Christian Church in Pendleton, Indiana, who allowed me to share this information as well.

There is also an old folklore that engineers can't write. Those who proofread my manuscripts, especially in its earliest forms, in an honest moment would probably agree with this statement. I want to express my sincere thanks and appreciation to those who took the time to read through my manuscript and provide me with feedback and corrections: my parents, Duane and June, my son and daughter, Tyler and Molly, my aunt Ann Whalen, my friend Maxine Wanger, and my brother in Christ, Bob Stevens. My heartfelt thanks to each of you.

A special thanks goes to my loving wife, Lonnie. Without her help and dedication, the completion of this book would not have been possible. She was a tireless sounding board, proofreader, and editor. Thank you.

Finally, a big thank you goes out to all of those who attended the various classes and sessions on this material, either in the church, in my home, or in other settings through the years. I am very grateful for your participation, feedback, and encouragement. I have seen transformed lives along the way, including conversions from other religions to Christianity, and I am humbled by what God can accomplish. You, and future recipients of this material, as well as my own curiosity, are why I have spent many hours digging, reading, researching, and now writing. May your lives be forever positively transformed, knowing we can have confidence in our faith in Jesus Christ.

Table of Figures

Introduction
Figure i.1: Speaking the same language without realizing it

Chapter 1: How Did It All Begin?
Figure 1.1: Sealed box with coffee setting
Figure 1.2: Sealed box with universe inside
Figure 1.3: Albert Einstein
Figure 1.4: Physicists Robert Wilson and Arno Penzias with their radio listening device in 1965
Figure 1.5: NASA's graphic representation of the big bang and expansion of the universe

Chapter 2: Creating the Perfect Biosphere for Life
Figure 2.1: Earth
Figure 2.2: Artist rendering of Milky Way

Chapter 3: How Did Life Begin?
Figure 3.1: Charles Darwin
Figure 3.2: Trilobite fossil from Cambrian Explosion
Figure 3.3: Darwinian evolution versus fossil record
Figure 3.4: Artist rendition of Cambrian Explosion life forms
Figure 3.5: Artist rendering of Tyrannosaurus rex
Figure 3.6: Mousetrap
Figure 3.7: Artist rendering of the human cell
Figure 3.8: Bacterial flagellum
Figure 3.9: DNA packaged as chromosome
Figure 3.10: Computer vs. DNA information storage

Chapter 4: Are We Physically Evolved Apes?
Figure 4.1: DNA strands
Figure 4.2: DNA replication

Chapter 6: What Yom Is It?
Figure 6.1: Grand Canyon
Figure 6.2: Elapsed time since the beginning of the universe
Figure 6.3: Length of each creation period
Figure 6.4: Time span of each creation period
Figure 6.5: Major creation events during the first six biblical yoms
Figure 6.6: Evolution-based population models
Figure 6.7: Decay in patriarchal life span following flood
Figure 6.8: Bible-based population model
Figure 6.9: Arlington National Cemetery

Chapter 7: Old Testament–Era Evidence
Figure 7.1: Periodic table of the elements
Figure 7.2: Modern-day Euphrates River
Figure 7.3: Mount Ararat in Turkey
Figure 7.4: Clay tablet dating to 600 BC depicting Tower of Babel
Figure 7.5: Restored bottom stories of a ziggurat from Abraham's home town of Ur
Figure 7.6: Gate of Hattusa, the Hittite capital
Figure 7.7: Ancient mud-brick pyramid at Hawara built by Pharaoh Amenemhet III
Figure 7.8: Christian communion meal
Figure 7.9: Mount Sinai
Figure 7.10: Sinai Desert
Figure 7.11: Ancient ruins from the city of Jericho
Figure 7.12: Ancient Tel Dan wall
Figure 7.13: Valley of Elah where David killed Goliath
Figure 7.14: Ruins from six-chambered gate at Hazor
Figure 7.15: Tel Beersheba ancient ruins
Figure 7.16: Moabite stone

Figure 7.17: Carved stone with inscription found along Siloam tunnel dating to 701 BC
Figure 7.18: Desolate ruins from ancient Babylon

Chapter 8: Prophecies on Jesus
Figure 8.1: Daniel 9:25 accurately predicts Jesus's coming 566 years in advance
Figure 8.2: Qumran caves where Dead Sea Scrolls were found
Figure 8.3: Dead Sea Scroll

Chapter 9: New Testament-Era Evidence
Figure 9.1: Modern-day Bethlehem
Figure 9.2: Modern-day Nazareth
Figure 9.3: Cana in Galilee
Figure 9.4: Remains of house believed to be that of the disciple Peter
Figure 9.5: Ruins of Capernaum synagogue where Jesus taught
Figure 9.6: 1894 photo of Jacob's well
Figure 9.7: Pool at Bethesda
Figure 9.8: Caesarea Philippi
Figure 9.9: Pool of Siloam in Jerusalem
Figure 9.10: Beth Shen (Scythopolis), one of the ten cities of the Decapolis
Figure 9.11: Stone found in Caesarea in 1961 with Pontius Pilate's name on it
Figure 9.12: Golgotha
Figure 9.13: Trenches cut in rock beneath Dome of the Rock match Bible dimensions for holy of holies
Figure 9.14: Church of the Holy Sepulcher
Figure 9.15: Ancient burial tomb in Jerusalem
Figure 9.16: Shroud of Turin
Figure 9.17: Theater from ancient Caesarea
Figure 9.18: Ruins at Antioch
Figure 9.19: Theater in Philippi
Figure 9.20: Theater in Ephesus

Figure 9.21: Theater in Thessalonica
Figure 9.22: Areopagus hill overlooking Athens
Figure 9.23: Jerusalem
Figure 9.24: Armageddon where the Bible states the final battle will take place

Endnotes

Chapter 1: How Did It All Begin?

1. Richard Panek, "The Year of Albert Einstein," *Smithsonian Magazine* (June 2005), www.smithsonianmag.com/science-nature/the-year-of-albert-einstein-75841381.
2. J.C. Hafele and Richard E. Keating, "Around-the-World Atomic Clocks: Predicted Relativistic Time Gains," Science, New Series, Vol. 177, No. 4044 (July 14, 1972), 166–168, www.uam.es/personal_pdi/ciencias/jcuevas/.../Hafele-Keating-Science-1972b.pdf.
3. Richard W. Pogge, "Real-World Relativity: The GPS Navigation System," Updated March 11, 2017, www.astronomy.ohio-state.edu/~pogge/Ast162/Unit5/gps.html.
4. Fred Heeren, *Show Me God*, (Day Star Publications, seventh printing, 2004), 140.
5. Heeren, *Show Me God*, 135.
6. Heeren, *Show Me God*, 151.
7. Heeren, *Show Me God*, 147.
8. Heeren, *Show Me God*, 135.
9. Fred Hoyle, *The Intelligent Universe*, (New York: Holt, Rinehart and Winston, 1983), 237.
10. Fred Heeren, *Show Me God*, (Day Star Publications, seventh printing, 2004), 153.
11. www.kingjamesbibleonline.org/Popular-Bible-Words.php.
12. "The Big Bang," Science Mission Directorate, Science @ NASA, https://science.nasa.gov/astrophysics/focus-areas/what-powered-the-big-bang.
13. "Origin of the Elements," August 9, 2000, www2.lbl.gov/abc/wallchart/chapters/10/0.html.
14. "How 'Fast' is the Speed of Light?" NASA, www.grc.nasa.gov/www/k-12/Numbers/Math/Mathematical_Thinking/how_fast_is_the_speed.htm.
15. "Universe Expansion Funnel," NASA, EMS: Universe, released September 20, 2016, https://svs.gsfc.nasa.gov/12314.

16. Bodie Hodgeand Terry Mortenson, "Did Moses Write Genesis?" Answers in Genesis, June 28, 2011, https://answersingenesis.org/bible-characters/moses/did-moses-write-genesis; Don Stewart, "When Did Moses Write, or Compile, the Book of Genesis?" www.blueletterbible.org/faq/don_stewart/don_stewart_678.cfm.

Chapter 2: Creating the Perfect Biosphere for Life

1. Jim Denney, "Why the Universe is Fine-Tuned for Life—Not Just 'Life As We Know It,'" God and Soul, https://godandsoul.wordpress.com/tag/fine-tuned-universe.
2. "The Universe: Past and Present Reflections," Engineering and Science, California Institute of Technology, November 1981, 12, http://calteches.library.caltech.edu/527/2/Hoyle.pdf.
3. Rich Deem, "Evidence for the Fine Tuning of the Universe," last modified May 17, 2011, www.godandscience.org/apologetics/designun.html.
4. Deem, "Evidence for Fine Tuning."
5. Lee Strobel, *The Case for a Creator*, (Zondervan, 2004), 131.
6. Steven Hawking, *A Brief History of Time*, (New York: Bantam Books, 1988), 125.
7. Carl Sagan, "The Search for Extraterrestrial Life," Scientific American, October 1994, 93.
8. Guillermo Gonzalez and Jay Richards, *The Privileged Planet*, (Regnery Publishing, Inc, 2004).
9. Lee Strobel, *The Case for a Creator*, (Zondervan, 2004), quote by G. Gonzalez, 170.
10. Lee Strobel, *The Case for a Creator*, (Zondervan, 2004), quote by G. Gonzalez, 173.
11. Tim Sharp, "How Far is Earth from the Sun?" Science & Astronomy, September 17, 2012, www.space.com/17081-how-far-is-earth-from-the-sun.html.
12. Lee Strobel, *The Case for a Creator*, (Zondervan, 2004), quote by G. Gonzalez, 175.
13. "Solar Variability and Terrestrial Climate," NASA, Science News, January 8, 2013, https://science.nasa.gov/science-news/science-at-nasa/2013/08jan_sunclimate.
14. Guillermo Gonzalez and Jay Richards, *The Privileged Planet*, (Regnery Publishing, Inc, 2004), 6.

15. Jacques Laskar, "The Moon and the Origin of Life on Earth," April 1993, www.imcce.fr/fr/presentation/equipes/ASD/person/Laskar/misc_files/PLS_amer.pdf.
16. Lee Strobel, *The Case for a Creator*, (Zondervan, 2004), quote by G. Gonzalez, 179.

Chapter 3: How Did Life Begin?

1. Jeffrey L Bada and Antonio Lazcana, "Stanley L. Miller," Biographical Memoir, National Academy of Sciences, 2012, www.nasonline.org/publications/biographical-memoirs/memoir-pdfs/miller-stanley.pdf.
2. Lee Strobel, *The Case for a Creator*, (Zondervan, 2004), quote by J. Wells, 37–38.
3. John Hopper "Mathematics & Evolution," 2016, 1, www.jkhlibrary.com/uploads/7/4/4/3/7443374/mathematics_and_evolution.pdf.
4. John Carl Villanueva, "How many atoms are there in the universe?" Universe Today, July 20, 2008, updated December 24, 2015, www.universetoday.com/36302/atoms-in-the-universe.
5. Charles Darwin, *The Origin of Species*, (Castle Books, 2004), 208.
6. Darwin, *Origin of Species*, 223–224.
7. Tia Ghose, "Evolutionary 'Big Bang' Was Triggered by Multiple Events," Live Science, September 19, 2013, www.livescience.com/39790-cambrian-explosion-had-multiple-causes.html.
8. "Preserving an exceptional fossil site for future generations," University of Oxford, Mathematical Physical and Life Sciences Division, www.mpls.ox.ac.uk/research-section/preserving-an-exceptional-fossil-site-for-future-generations; James W. Valentine, David Jablonski, and Douglas H. Erwin, "Fossils, molecules and embryos: new perspectives on the Cambrian explosion," The Company of Biologists Limited, 1999. Development 126, pp. 851–859, http://lepdata.org/monteiro/Evo-devo%20pdfs/Valentine%20et%20al.%201999.pdf.
9. "Timeline of the evolutionary history of life," https://en.wikipedia.org/wiki/Timeline_of_the_evolutionary_history_of_life.
10. "Timeline of evolutionary history."
11. "Who Discovered the First Dinosaur Bone?" 2014–2017 National Center for Families Learning August 18, 2016, https://wonderopolis.org/wonder/who-discovered-the-first-dinosaur-bone.

12. Keith Robison, "Darwin's Black Box: Irreducible Complexity or Irreproducible Irreducibility?" 1996–1997, last update December 11, 1996, http://www.talkorigins.org/faqs/behe/review.html.
13. Lee Strobel, *The Case for a Creator*, (Zondervan, 2004), quote by M. Behe, 205.
14. "The Francis Crick Papers: The Discovery of the Double Helix, 1951–1953," US National Library of Medicine, https://profiles.nlm.nih.gov/ps/retrieve/Narrative/SC/p-nid/143.
15. "How Long is Your DNA?" Science Focus, July 28, 2011, www.sciencefocus.com/qa/how-long-your-dna.
16. Alan McDougall, "What are the Odds of Life evolving by chance alone?" Evolution, Morphology and Exobiology, July 22, 2012, www.scienceforums.net/topic/67884-what-are-the-odds-of-life-evolving-by-chance-alone.
17. Fred Heeren, *Show Me God*, (Day Star Publications, seventh printing, 2004), 209.

Chapter 4: Are We Physically Evolved Apes?

1. "Timeline of human evolution," Wikipedia, October 3, 2017, https://en.wikipedia.org/wiki/Timeline_of_human_evolution.
2. Evan Andrews, "Famed 'Lucy' Fossils Discovered in Ethiopa, 40 Years Ago," History, November 24, 2014, www.history.com/news/famed-lucy-fossils-discovered-in-ethiopia-40-years-ago.
3. "Java Man, First Human Missing Link Fossil?" Darwin, Then and Now, May 15, 2012, www.darwinthenandnow.com/2012/05/java-man-first-human-missing-link-fossil.
4. Bert Thompson, "Neanderthal Man – Another Look," Apologetics Press, 2017, www.apologeticspress.org/apcontent.aspx?category=9&article=625.
5. "Cro-Magnon Anthropology," Encyclopedia Britannica, www.britannica.com/topic/Cro-Magnon.
6. "Denisovan," Wikipedia, last edited September 27, 2017, https://en.wikipedia.org/wiki/Denisovan.
7. Fazala Rana, "The Leap to Two Feet: The Sudden Appearance of Bipedalism," Reasons to Believe, October 1, 2001, www.reasons.org/articles/the-leap-to-two-feet-the-sudden-appearance-of-bipedalism.
8. Carlos Bustamente and Fernando Mendez, "Modern Men Lack Y Chromosome Genes from Neanderthals," Stanford Medicine, News

Center, April 17, 2016, https://med.stanford.edu/news/all-news/2016/04/modern-men-lack-y-chromosome-genes-from-neanderthals.html.

9. "Timeline: Organisms that have had their genome sequenced," Wellcome Genome Campus, Facts, last updated January 19, 2015, www.yourgenome.org/facts/timeline-organisms-that-have-had-their-genomes-sequenced.
10. "All About the Human Genome Promject (HGP)," National Human Genome Research Institute, last updated October 1, 2015, www.genome.gov/10001772/all-about-the--human-genome-project-hgp.
11. David DeWitt, "Chip Genome Very Different from Man," Answers in Genesis, September 5, 2005, https://answersingenesis.org/genetics/dna-similarities/chimp-genome-sequence-very-different-from-man.
12. Jennifer Hughes, et al, "Chimpanzee and human Y chromosomes are remarkably divergent in structure and gene content," Nature 463, 536–539, January 20, 2010, www.nature.com/nature/journal/v463/n7280/abs/nature08700.html?foxtrotcallback=true.
13. Thomas J. Parson, "A high observed substitution rate in the human mitochondrial DNA control region," Nature Publishing Group, 1997, Nature Genetics 15, 363–368, www.nature.com/ng/journal/v15/n4/abs/ng0497-363.html.
14. Nathaniel T. Jeanson, "A Young-Earth Creation Human Mitochrondrial DNA 'Clock': Whole Mitochrondrial Genome Mutation Rate Confirms D-Loop Results," Answers in Genesis, September 23, 2015, https://answersingenesis.org/genetics/mitochondrial-genome-mutation-rate.
15. Jacon A. Tennessen, et al, "Evolution and Functional Impact of Rare Coding Variation from Deep Sequencing of Human Exomes," Science, July 16, 2012, vol. 337, issue 6090, 64–69, http://science.sciencemag.org/content/337/6090/64.
16. John C. Sanford and Robert Carter, "In Light of Genetics … Adam, Eve and the Creation/Fall," Christian Apologetics Journal, 2014, www.galaxie.com/article/caj12-2-04.
17. Lydia Ramsey and Samantha Lee, "Our DNA is 99.9% the same as the person sitting next to us—and we're surprisingly similar to a bunch of other living things," Business Insider, May 6, 2016, www.businessinsider.com/comparing-genetic-similarity-between-humans-and-other-things-2016-5.

Chapter 5: Are We Spiritually Evolved Apes?

1. "Cogito, ergo, sum," Encyclopedia Britannica, 2017, www.britannica.com/topic/cogito-ergo-sum.
2. Michael Ruse, *Can a Darwinian Be a Christian?* (Cambridge: Oxford University Press, 2001), 73.
3. Lee Strobel, *The Case for a Creator*, (Zondervan, 2004), thoughts by J.P. Moreland, 255–256.
4. "Wilder Penfield 1891–1976," A Science Odyssey: People and Discoveries: Wilder Penfield, PBS, 1998, www.pbs.org/wgbh/aso/databank/entries/bhpenf.html.
5. Tara MacIsaac, "How Common Are Near-Death Experiences? NDE's by the Numbers," The Epoch Times, June 23, 2014, www.theepochtimes.com/how-common-are-near-death-experiences-ndes-by-the-numbers_757401.html.
6. "Near-death experiences? Results of the world's largest medical study of the human mind and consciousness at time of death," Science Daily, University of Southampton, October 7, 2014, www.sciencedaily.com/releases/2014/10/141007092108.htm.
7. "Dr. Kenneth Ring's Near-Death Experience Research," Near Death Experiences and the Afterlife, 2014, www.near-death.com/science/experts/kenneth-ring.html.
8. "Dr. Melvin Morse's Near-Death Experience Research," Near Death Experiences and the Afterlife, 2017, www.near-death.com/science/experts/melvin-morse.html.
9. Lee Strobel, *The Case for a Creator*, (Zondervan, 2004), 251.
10. Kevin Williams, "People Have Near-Death Experiences While Brain Dead," Near Death Experiences and the Afterlife, 2017, www.near-death.com/science/evidence/people-have-ndes-while-brain-dead.html.
11. "The Cuneiform Writing System in Ancient Mesopotamia: Emergence and Evolution," National Endowment for the Humanities, http://edsitement.neh.gov/lesson-plan/cuneiform-writing-system-ancient-mesopotamia-emergence-and-evolution.
12. Megan Gambino, "A Salute to the Wheel," Smithsonian.com, June 17, 2009, www.smithsonianmag.com/science-nature/a-salute-to-the-wheel-31805121.

Chapter 6: What Yom Is It?

1. Greg Neyman, "Word Study: Yom," Old Earth Creation Science, Old Earth Ministries, 2007, March 16, 2005, www.oldearth.org/word_study_yom.htm.
2. Neyman, "Word Study: Yom."
3. Rich Deem, "No Death Before the Fall—A Young Earth Problem," God and Science, last updated November 13, 2013, www.godandscience.org/youngearth/death.html.
4. "How Old is the Universe?" NASA, updated December 21, 2013, https://map.gsfc.nasa.gov/universe/uni_age.html.
5. "Gallery: Universe's Cosmic Microwave Background Revealed by Planck Observatory," SPACE.com staff, March 21, 2013, www.space.com/20332-cosmic-microwave-background-planck-discoveries-images.html.
6. Glenn Elert, "Half-Life of Carbon-14," The Physics Factbook, 1997, https://hypertextbook.com/facts/1997/MargaretKong.shtml.
7. "Continental Drift," Encyclopedia Britannica, 2017, www.britannica.com/science/continental-drift-geology.
8. "Unlocking Secrets of the Grand Canyon's Age," National Geographic, January 26, 2014, http://news.nationalgeographic.com/news/2014/01/140126-grand-canyon-american-southwest-erosion-geology-geophysics.
9. Holli Riebeck, "Paleoclimatology: The Ice Core Record," NASA, December 19, 2005, https://earthobservatory.nasa.gov/Features/Paleoclimatology_IceCores.
10. D.E. Wonderly, "Coral Reefs and Related Carbonate Structures as Indicators of Great Age," Inter-Disciplinary Biblical Research Institute, Report No. 16, 1983, www.ibri.org/Tracts/reefstct.htm.
11. Ben Raines, "Alabama's 60,000-year-old underwater forests spills its secrets in new documentary," Alabama Media Group, updated September 25, 2017.
12. "Bristlecone Pine," National Park Service, US Department of Interior, updated February 24, 2015, www.nps.gov/brca/learn/nature/bristleconepine.htm.
13. "World Population Clock," Worldometers, September 9, 2017, www.worldometers.info/world-population.
14. Eric R. Pianka, "Land," University of Texas, www.zo.utexas.edu/courses/thoc/land.html.

15. "Facts on Arlington National Cemetery," WETA, 2017, https://weta.org/press/facts-arlington-national-cemetery.

Chapter 7: Old Testament–Era Evidence

1. "Adam's Rib," Genesis and Genetics, November 5, 2001, www.genesisandgenetics.org/2011/11/05/adams-rib.
2. Michael Brown, "Mitochondrial Eve," Molecular History Research Center, last revised January 6, 2017, www.mhrc.net/mitochondrialEve.htm.
3. "Bronze Age," Merriam-Webster Dictionary, www.merriam-webster.com/dictionary/Bronze%20Age.
4. Monty White, "Flood Legends. The Significance of a World of Stories Based on Truth," Answers in Genesis, March 29, 2007, https://answersingenesis.org/the-flood/flood-legends/flood-legends.
5. John Noble Wilford, "Plumbing Black Sea for Proof of the Deluge," *New York Times*, January 5, 1999, www.nytimes.com/1999/01/05/science/plumbing-black-sea-for-proof-of-the-deluge.html.
6. Andrew A. Snelling, "How Did We Get All This Coal?" Answers in Genesis, April 1, 2013, https://answersingenesis.org/biology/plants/how-did-we-get-all-this-coal.
7. Dave Balsiger and Charles E. Sellier Jr., *In Search of Noah's Ark*, Sun Classic Pictures, Inc., (1976), 2.
8. Ann Gibbons, "Calibrating the Mitochondrial Clock," First International Workshop on Human Mitochondrial DNA, 25 to 28 October 1997, Washington, D.C., American Association for the Advancement of Science, Science 279, 28–29.
9. Nathaniel T. Jeanson, "On the Origin of Human Mitochondrial DNA Differences, New Generation Time Data Both Suggest a Unified Young-Earth Creation Model and Challenge the Evolutionary Out-of-Africa Model," Answers in Genesis, April 27, 2016, https://answersingenesis.org/genetics/mitochondrial-dna/origin-human-mitochondrial-dna-differences-new-generation-time-data-both-suggest-unified-young-earth.
10. Anugrah Kumar, "Evidence for Bible's Tower of Babel Discovered," The Christian Post, May 9, 2017, www.christianpost.com/news/evidence-bible-tower-of-babel-discovered-183038.
11. Sinan Salaheddin, "Home of Abraham, Ur, unearthed by archaeologists in Iraq," The Christian Science Monitor, Associated

Press, April 4, 2013, www.csmonitor.com/Science/2013/0404/Home-of-Abraham-Ur-unearthed-by-archaeologists-in-Iraq.
12. Bert Thompson, "Biblical Accuracy and Circumcision on the 8th Day," Apologetics Press, 1993, http://apologeticspress.org/apcontent.aspx?category=13&article=1118.
13. "Convince Me There's a God – Archaeology 2," Faith and Self Defense, August 6, 2013, https://faithandselfdefense.com/2013/08/06/convince-me-theres-a-god-archaeology-2.
14. David Down, "The Pyramids of Ancient Egypt," Answers in Genesis, September 1, 2004, https://answersingenesis.org/archaeology/ancient-egypt/the-pyramids-of-ancient-egypt.
15. "Mernepthah Stele," All About Archaeology, 2017, www.allaboutarchaeology.org/merneptah-stele-faq.htm.
16. Scott Ashely and Jerold Aust, "Jericho: Does the Evidence Disprove or Prove the Bible?" Associates for Bible Research, January 30, 2009, www.biblearchaeology.org/post/2009/01/Jericho-Does-the-Evidence-Disprove-or-Prove-the-Bible.aspx.
17. Jeff A. Benner, "Ugarit and the Bible," Ancient Hebrew Research Center, 2017, www.ancient-hebrew.org/bible_ugarit.html.
18. "Ancient Israel," All About the Journey, 2017, www.allaboutthejourney.org/ancient-israel.htm.
19. Ray Vander Laan, "The High Place and Altar at Dan," That the World May Know, Focus on the Family, 2017, www.thattheworldmayknow.com/the-high-place-and-altar-at-dan.
20. Kristin Romey, "Discovery of Philistine Cemetery May Solve Biblical Mystery," National Geographic, July 10, 2016, http://news.nationalgeographic.com/2016/07/bible-philistine-israelite-israel-ashkelon-discovery-burial-archaeology-sea-peoples.
21. "The Tel Dan inscription: The First Historical Evidence of King David from the Bible," Bible History Daily, Biblical Archaeology Society Staff, November 8, 2016, www.biblicalarchaeology.org/daily/biblical-artifacts/artifacts-and-the-bible/the-tel-dan-inscription-the-first-historical-evidence-of-the-king-david-bible-story.
22. "Biblical Archaeology 2: The Pool at Gibeon," Theo-sopical Ruminations, July 13, 2011, https://theosophical.wordpress.com/2011/07/13/biblical-archaeology-2-the-pool-at-gibeon.
23. Taman Turbinton, "A History of the Land and Archaeology of Gezer," Discerning History, May 18, 2016, http://discerninghistory.com/2016/05/a-history-of-the-land-and-archaeology-of-gezer.

24. "Archaeology in Israel: Ancient City of Beersheba," Jewish Virtual Library, American-Israeli Cooperative Enterprise, 2017, www.jewishvirtuallibrary.org/ancient-city-of-beersheba.
25. "The Moabite Stone," Bible History Online, www.bible-history.com/resource/ff_mesha.htm.
26. "Biblical Archaeology 8: The Black Obelisk of Shalmaneser," Theo-sophical Ruminations, August 2, 2011, https://theosophical.wordpress.com/2011/08/02/biblical-archaeology-8-the-black-obelisk-of-shalmaneser.
27. "King Uzziah in Archeology," Bible Reading Archeology, January 11, 2016, https://biblereadingarcheology.com/2016/01/11/king-uzziah.
28. Christopher Rollston, "The Siloam Inscription and Hezekiah's Tunnel," Bible Odyssey, Society of Bible Literature, 2017, www.bibleodyssey.org/en/places/related-articles/siloam-inscription-and-hezekiahs-tunnel.
29. "The Babylonian Chronicle (Chronicle 5): Nebuchadnezzar Besieges Jersualem, 597 BCE," Center for Online Judaic Studies, 2017, http://cojs.org/the_babylonian_chronicle_-chronicle_5-_nebuchadnezzar_besieges_jerusalem-_597_bce.
30. Ginger Yapp, "The Ruins of Babylon," *USA Today*, http://traveltips.usatoday.com/ruins-babylon-54842.html.
31. Dave Miller, "There is Still Hope for Israel," Apologetics Press, 1986, www.apologeticspress.org/APContent.aspx?category=7&article=4186&topic=324.

Chapter 8: Prophecies on Jesus

1. Wayne Jackson, "How Many Prophecies Are in the Bible?" ChristianCourier.com, October 13, 2017, www.christiancourier.com/articles/318-how-many-prophecies-are-in-the-bible.
2. "353 Prophecies Fulfilled in Jesus Christ," Accordingtothescriptures.org, 2015, www.accordingtothescriptures.org/prophecy/353prophecies.html.
3. "When was the Bible written?" This is YOUR Bible, 2015, www.thisisyourbible.com/index.php?page=questions&task=show&mediaid=965.
4. "The Dead Sea Scrolls—Discovery and Publications," The Leon Levy Dead Sea Scrolls Digital Library, Israel Antiquities Authority, 2012, www.deadseascrolls.org.il/learn-about-the-scrolls/discovery-and-publication?locale=en_US.

5. John Nuyten, "Dead Sea Scrolls," Different Spirit.org, 2017, www.differentspirit.org/evidence/dead-sea-scrolls.php.
6. Norman Geisler, "Has the Bible Been Accurately Copied Down Through the Centuries?" Southern Evangelical Seminary & Bible College, 2016, https://ses.edu/has-the-bible-been-accurately-copied-down-through-the-centuries.

Chapter 9: New Testament–Era Evidence

1. "Bronze Bust of Augustus," Bible History Online. www.bible-history.com/archaeology/rome/bronze-augustus.html.
2. "Church of the Nativity, Bethlehem," Sacred Destination, 2017, www.sacred-destinations.com/israel/bethlehem-church-of-the-nativity.
3. "Dionysius Exiguus," Encyclopedia.com, The Gale Group Inc., 2001, www.encyclopedia.com/science/encyclopedias-almanacs-transcripts-and-maps/dionysius-exiguus
4. "Biblical Archaeology 38: Peter's House in Capernaum," Theo-sophical Ruminations, September 16, 2011, https://theosophical.wordpress.com/2011/09/16/biblical-archaeology-38-peter%E2%80%99s-house-in-capernaum.
5. "Capernaum, Galilee," Israeljerusalem.com, 2017, www.israeljerusalem.com/capernaum-israel.htm.
6. "Archaeology and the Bible: New Testament," Stock # 432X, Rose Publishing, 2003.
7. "Jacob's Well," See the Holy Land, 2017, www.seetheholyland.net/jacobs-well.
8. "Pool of Bethesada," AllAboutArchaeology.org, 2017, www.allaboutarchaeology.org/pool-of-bethesda-faq.htm.
9. Brad Harrub, "The Discovery of the Siloam Pool," Apologetics Press, 2005, www.apologeticspress.org/apcontent.aspx?category=13&article=1476.
10. "Decapolis," Christian Archaeology Sites, Christian Tours, September 4, 2010, https://dannythedigger.com/christian_archaeology/decapolis.
11. "Biblical Archaeology 36: Lysanias Inscription," Theo-sophical Ruminations, September 15, 2011, https://theosophical.wordpress.com/2011/09/15/biblical-archaeology-36-lysanias-inscription.
12. Titus Kennedy, "The Archaeology of a Trial," Hope Channel, September 2, 2015, www.hopechannel.com/read/the-archaeology-of-a-trial.
13. "Pontius Pilate," AllAboutArcheaology.org, 2017, www.allaboutarchaeology.org/pontius-pilate-faq.htm.

14. "The Location of the Temple and the Holy of Holies on the Temple Mount," Temple Mount and Land of Israel Faithful Movement, 2017, www.templemountfaithful.org/articles/temple-location.php.
15. Ron J. Bigalke, "Is It possible to know where Christ was buried?" Christian Apologetics and Research Ministry, October 11, 2012, https://carm.org/is-it-possible-to-know-where-christ-was-buried.
16. Shroud of Turin Education and Research Association, Inc. www.shroud.com/stera.htm.
17. Mark Guscin, "The Sudarium of Oviedo: Its History and Relationship to the Shroud of Turin," Shroud of Turin Education and Research Association, Inc., 1997.
18. "Archaeology and the Bible: New Testament," Rose Publishing, 2003.
19. "Antioch, Turkey," Sacred Destinations, http://www.sacred-destinations.com/turkey/antioch
20. "Sergius Paulus," www.BibleHistory.net, 2013, www.biblehistory.net/newsletter/paulus.htm.
21. "The Erastus inscription at Corinth," Ferrell's Travel Blog, October 23, 2013, https://ferrelljenkins.wordpress.com/2013/10/23/the-erastus-inscription-at-corinth.
22. "The Tribute Penny," Dirty Old Coins, April 24, 2014, http://dirtyoldcoins.com/Roman-Coins-Blog/2016/4/23/the-tribute-penny.
23. "Armageddon," Bible Study Tools, 2017, www.biblestudytools.com/dictionary/armageddon.

Chapter 10: Did the Resurrection Really Happen?

1. Matt Perman, "Historical Evidence for the Resurrection," Desiring God, September 12, 2007, www.desiringgod.org/articles/historical-evidence-for-the-resurrection.
2. J. Warner Wallace, "Is There Any Evidence for Jesus Outside of the Bible?" Cold Case Christianity, 2017, http://coldcasechristianity.com/2014/is-there-any-evidence-for-jesus-outside-the-bible.
3. "TITUS FLAVIUS JOSEPHUS," Land of the Bible, 2016, www.land-of-the-bible.com/Titus_Flavius_Josephus.

Chapter 11: What Have Others Written about Jesus?

1. William Lane Craig, "Thallus on the Darkness at Noon," Reasonable Faith, www.reasonablefaith.org/thallus-on-the-darkness-at-noon.
2. "TITUS FLAVIUS JOSEPHUS," Land of the Bible, 2016, www.land-of-the-bible.com/Titus_Flavius_Josephus.
3. "TITUS FLAVIUS JOSEPHUS."
4. Warner J. Wallace, "Is There Any Evidence for Jesus Outside of the Bible?" Cold Case Christianity, 2017, http://coldcasechristianity.com/2014/is-there-any-evidence-for-jesus-outside-the-bible.
5. Wallace, "Evidence Outside Bible."
6. Wallace, "Evidence Outside Bible."
7. Wallace, "Evidence Outside Bible."
8. Peter Kirby, "Pliny the Younger: Pliny the Younger and Trajan on the Christians," Early Christian Writings, 2017, www.earlychristianwritings.com/text/pliny.html.
9. "Tactius on the Christians," Livius.org, November 29, 2015, www.livius.org/sources/content/tacitus/tacitus-on-the-christians.
10. J. Warner J. Wallace, "Is There Any Evidence for Jesus Outside of the Bible?" Cold Case Christianity, 2017, http://coldcasechristianity.com/2014/is-there-any-evidence-for-jesus-outside-the-bible.
11. Wallace, "Evidence Outside Bible."
12. Wallace, "Evidence Outside Bible."
13. Wallace, "Evidence Outside Bible."
14. Wallace, "Evidence Outside Bible."
15. Wallace, "Evidence Outside Bible."
16. Wallace, "Evidence Outside Bible."